It's Not My Fault

It's Not My Fault

*Victim Mentality and
Becoming Response-able*

George A. Goens

ROWMAN & LITTLEFIELD
Lanham • Boulder • New York • London

Published by Rowman & Littlefield
A wholly owned subsidiary of The Rowman & Littlefield Publishing Group, Inc.
4501 Forbes Boulevard, Suite 200, Lanham, Maryland 20706
www.rowman.com

Unit A, Whitacre Mews, 26-34 Stannary Street, London SE11 4AB

Copyright © 2017 by George A. Goens

All rights reserved. No part of this book may be reproduced in any form or by any electronic or mechanical means, including information storage and retrieval systems, without written permission from the publisher, except by a reviewer who may quote passages in a review.

British Library Cataloguing in Publication Information Available

Library of Congress Cataloging-in-Publication Data

978-1-4758-3385-0 (cloth : alk. paper)
978-1-4758-3386-7 (pbk. : alk. paper)
978-1-4758-3387-4 (electronic)

∞ ™ The paper used in this publication meets the minimum requirements of American National Standard for Information Sciences Permanence of Paper for Printed Library Materials, ANSI/NISO Z39.48-1992.

Printed in the United States of America

For
Marilyn—a resilient and loving optimist
Betsy—an enthusiastic and compassionate daughter who is missed every day
Curtis—a son who is a steadfast professional and father serving the common good
Betty—a resilient and loving sister
Teachers—significant polestars providing children with loving care, understanding, and guidance

Contents

Preface	ix
Acknowledgments	xiii
1 More Than Academics	1
2 Students and Victim Mentality	11
3 Response-able or Passive Victim?	25
4 Victim Mentality and Life	33
5 Character Matters	45
6 Being and Self-Efficacy	59
7 Teachers, Schools, and Responsibility	71
8 Parents, Children, and Responsibility	87
9 Flourish or Languish	99
10 Managing Life	107
11 What Is at Stake?	117
Bibliography	125
Index	129

Preface

All children have hopes and dreams. The innocent optimism of children from their early years to working their way through school is inspiring. While they may eventually cast off childhood ambitions of being athletic superstars or famous actors, they still have dreams as they mature and face life.

The foundation of the United States is based on aspirations and the ideal called the "American Dream" that beckons all to freely pursue their goals and hopes. It is founded on values and an ethos that is unique in history. Individualism, supported by the beliefs of liberty, equality, justice, and the common good, has been at the core of the American spirit. The United States has always been perceived as the "land of opportunity."

Our society expects children to learn, adopt, and respond to these ideals and apply their talent, effort, and creativity for the best in life. These values are of particular importance in how individuals approach life and its challenges, as well as how we raise and educate our children.

Our society and government are based upon optimism that drives all aspects of our culture and lives. In that regard, every citizen should have an equal opportunity to pursue success and meaning by participating actively, accepting responsibility, and working hard. Our society honors determination and celebrates individuals who have taken the initiative to innovate and succeed.

The United States is based upon the foundation of democracy, equal rights, independence, and opportunity. All of these values require action, dedication, and involvement; they do not rely on paternalism, economic privilege, or royal standing. They are prerequisites and motivating forces for achievement and upward mobility, but their application rests in our individual hands as conscientious and determined citizens.

In two simple phrases, the Declaration of Independence defines us. "All men are created equal" and "life, liberty, and the pursuit of happiness" describe the fundamentals of the "American Dream," a term coined by author and historian James Truslow Adams. In his 1931 book, *The Epic of America*, he wrote:

> That dream of a land in which life should be better and richer and fuller for everyone, with opportunity for each according to ability or achievement. . . . It is not a dream of motor cars and high wages merely, but a dream of social order in which each man and each woman shall be able to attain to the fullest stature of which they are innately capable, and be recognized by others for what they are, regardless of the fortuitous circumstances of birth or position.[1]

The American Dream is not simply about wealth or advancement. Personal fulfillment, finding meaning, and persevering are at its core. The dream is about freedom to commit—the ability to set a course and direct the path of life.

Fulfilling the American Dream is not something others hand to us. The word *dream* may be a misnomer because when we dream, we have little control over the exact content and images. We are asleep. In reality, the drive to find the fullest meaning of our lives is up to us, and it is not always easy.

The pursuit of happiness rests directly on the shoulders of individuals who are able to make decisions and assume responsibility to find purpose in life and achieve success. Happiness is realized through resolve and individual commitment.

Citizens' lives are driven through self-reliance. In other countries, the stereotypes of Americans really define this concept. The terms *individual*, *independent*, *self-reliant*, *competitive*, and *achievers* are frequently used to describe us. Freedom and America are almost synonymous. Self-made and independent are embedded in our cultural history and stories.

America is a positive and buoyant place of individual opportunity to stand up, speak out, and solve problems. The settling of the West, the rugged individualism, and the celebration of the "common man" all rested on the adeptness to meet obligations through responsible action.

Not all Americans believe the American Dream is alive. In one poll, six in ten citizens thought it is dead.[2] Some have experienced economic and social hopelessness and feel powerless to address their circumstances. They feel disenfranchised and believe they have lost the power to direct their lives. In some cases, they think the government should be more involved to ensure they have a fighting chance to pursue their aspirations. In other situations, they feel society and government placed hedgerows in their way that hampered their ability to find success.

Significant social or economic obstacles exist for some citizens. Some individuals, however, place self-induced and self-destructive obstacles in their own way. Moving out of complacency and helplessness requires belief, action, and adherence to the idea of self-efficacy.

Americans overall believe that a strong work ethic and a good education are the cornerstones for achieving the "dream." In addition, children need parents, teachers, and others to teach them the values of responsibility and persistence.

The aspiration of all parents and grandparents for their children is to have a good life, to experience success, to be independent, and to gain happiness. Happiness is achieved through commitment to discover one's calling and use one's talent and character in a significant way. The goal is to find fulfillment through passion and conviction.

Life does not follow a typical, formulaic Hollywood script. Generally, the protagonist lives happily ever after with a clear mind and no residue or complications: all within ninety minutes. The song "Bright Side of the Road" plays at the end. Problems are solved and happiness endures!

In real life, however, change, loss, tragedy, and events far beyond direct control happen; some situations of an individual's own making create dilemmas, pain, and failure. Other circumstances are uncontrollable beyond grasp and extremely powerful. Fate intervenes.

In all circumstances, however, there are "controllables" that we can influence. We have the power to interpret and respond to all events, whether self-created or provoked through social, political, or other forces.

In either event, all of us are "response-able"—able to respond and act ethically and morally to address conditions. With children, adults have to ensure that they develop the character and education to be able to react even in the darkest of times. Mature individuals do so; they do not adopt a self-destructive victim mentality.

As John Gardner stated in his classic book *Excellence*, children must continue to learn "not to engage in self-destructive behavior. We learn not to burn up energy and anxiety. We learn to manage our tensions if we have any, which we do. We learn that self-pity and resentment are among the most toxic of drugs, and if we get addicted we must break the habit at all costs."[3]

This book addresses the responsibilities of educators and parents in helping children in being "response-able" in actively facing the challenges of life. While we want our children to experience success, we also know that it is not predetermined or written in the stars. A victim mentality and learned helplessness eliminate any hope of successfully meeting their aspirations and dreams.

Children face obstacles—some are daunting and others are the normal ups and downs of childhood. Parents, schools, and others have an obligation to help children grow into maturity and learn that they can act in positive and sensible ways in good as well as in hard times. Sitting back is not the American way or emblematic of character.

To reject the ability to live a life we have imagined or dreamed results in a life lost, along with its potential and possibilities. We all have only one life to live, and we are able to respond to achieve an imagined life.

NOTES

1. James Truslow Adams, *The Epic of America* (New Brunswick, NJ: Transaction, 2012), 214–15.
2. Suzanne Lucas, "How to Achieve the American Dream," CBS MoneyWatch, June 6, 2004, http://www.cbsnews.com/news/how-to-revive-your-american-dream/.
3. John Gardner, *Excellence* (New York: W. W. Norton and Company, 1984), 127.

Acknowledgments

I would like to acknowledge Claire Bower and Bruce Dierbeck for their contributions to this book. I also want to thank Barbara Hunt and Marilyn Goens for their assistance with the formation and proofing of the text and resources.

OTHER ROWMAN & LITTLEFIELD BOOKS
BY GEORGE A. GOENS

Leadership for Hard Times
Resilient Leadership for Turbulent Times
Straitjacket: How Overregulation Stifles Creativity and Innovation in Education
The Fog of Reform

Chapter One

More Than Academics

"The school should be the main source of strength in a free society. Its job is the highest possible development of the individual in terms of his or her skills, the appreciation of the art of living, the ability to take part in the final decisions being made by his community and by the nation itself. In short, the school should be the key connecting link between the natural capacity of young people and their actual and potential achievements." —Norman Cousins

"You are missing a big chunk of development if you focus only on curriculum, instruction and assessment because there is much, much more to being successful in this world." —James P. Comer

Education is a prerequisite for living life to the fullest. Helping children to understand who they are, to develop their philosophy, and to discover their interests, talents, and ambitions are essential goals of a quality education.

Well-educated people revere knowledge and apply values and principles to guide them as they seek a meaningful life. They learn to make wise decisions premised on strong ethical and moral ideals and broad academic understanding.

All children, rich and poor, must be educated so they can contribute to the common good through responsible and active citizenship and adapt to changing times. Thinking critically, posing questions, as well as seeking answers and understanding and developing an ethical and moral framework are a part of being well-educated. Strong academic skills are essential, but children also need the values and principles that will form the foundation for their life's decisions.

An educated citizenry is essential to maintaining and growing our society and its values and institutions. Students must learn and reflect on our common values. Understanding customs, language, and respect for others in communication and relationships is important to a civil society. Acceptance of others from different social or economic strata or races or ethnicities is a significant part of the fabric of American life.

Education is a lifelong process of continuous learning and reflection. A sense of stewardship and a concern for the common good, not simply tending to self-interest or ego needs, are qualities required for mature and conscientious conduct.

Life is not simply a cognitive exercise of engineering and analyzing. It is much more complex. Rational plans fall by the wayside as the unexpected and intangible motivate and push events and conditions. People do not always behave in algorithmic fashion, and education is beyond what standardized tests can measure. When emotions flare, logic does not always prevail.

In this complex context, adults must have a conception of societal rules, culture, values, and principles. Ethical questions and issues are prominent in life as politics, economics, and innovations raise conflict and questions.

Being successful requires complex thinking: the ability to critically and skeptically evaluate ideas, concepts, theories, and philosophies. Students must learn to think creatively and be able to analyze, synthesize, and assess information and data. Understanding political and cultural values, as well as mastering knowledge and academic content, form the basis for active involvement as a citizen.

Discovering and exploring concepts is at the core of participating in and contributing to life. The common good requires individuals who think in order to research and sustain ideas and principles that are essential for them personally and for their families, as well as the greater good.

When all is said and done, education is about ideas, and from those ideas come decisions and action. "Not to engage in this pursuit of ideas is to live like ants instead of like men. The ant can live without ideas because the whole course of its life is fixed. But man has the freedom—and, therefore, the necessity—to choose and to choose in terms of ideas."[1]

Parents realize that the road traveled by their children is not always going to be smooth. Setbacks will occur and difficult choices will have to be made. Parental and adult support is important, but children have to learn how to traverse that road, which includes both achievement and loss. Parents cannot always be backseat drivers because they curtail independence and foster anxiety and insecurity that can lead children in the wrong direction and eclipse their sense of purpose.

A study by the Pew Research Center found widespread agreement among parents of all economic and social backgrounds concerning the traits children should be taught.[2] Responsibility was overwhelmingly cited by 94 percent of the parents as the most important trait, followed by hard work at 92 percent. Helpfulness, good manners, and independence were also deemed as highly important. As children grow into their teen years, independence was considered increasingly important.

This parental perspective is important and undergirds the mission of schools and the values behind an education. A comprehensive education certainly involves academic content and cognitive analysis, but it also includes learning values and principles that guide priorities and judgment. Knowledge, comprehension, and skills are important, but ethics, values, and character are an essential part of what parents cited in the Pew study. A universal aspiration of parents is for their children to be "good" and responsible people who can confront the changes they will inevitably experience.

Today's penchant for data, metrical analysis, and standardized testing in schools has distorted what an education really is and how schools operate. Basically, adults are not the sum of their tenth-grade standardized test or the ACT/SAT exams. Life and living are much more complex than that. "Standardized measures can limit the development of competence by driving curricula toward narrow demands of test preparation instead of allowing teachers to immerse students in complex problem solving and rich use of language."[3]

Actually, public education has always been more than simple recall of information. To paraphrase William Butler Yeats, education is not filling a bucket—it is the lighting of a fire. The fire is purpose, meaning, and commitment: all necessary for individual and social progress. Horace Mann emphasized that teaching democratic values sustains a civil society through individual responsibility, justice, equality, and goodness. Learning content and concepts requires critical and skeptical thinking based on philosophy, values, and ethics that direct thought and honorable action.

EDUCATION AND AMERICAN IDEALS

From its inception, America's founders, particularly Thomas Jefferson, understood the indispensable role public education plays in government, self-rule, and society. To succeed and thrive, the United States requires well-educated, high-minded people of courage.

Educators are concerned with children's academic performance but also their behavior, attitudes, and socioemotional development. In the long haul, character development, coupled with strong values and ethics, ensures a child's ability to become what is stereotypically called a mature "lifelong" learner and citizen.

Understanding and committing to principles and standards are essential if individuals are to be successful and traverse the dilemmas of life. Apathy and victimhood are not American traits—individuals must meet their responsibilities to themselves and their community.

Cognitive ability and values and beliefs are tied to character and personal, social, and political decisions. As former senator Gary Hart stated, "Values produce beliefs; beliefs are the source of principles; principles are the basis of ideology; ideology produces policies; policies are the foundation of programs. There is, in other words, a logic to the development of ideas that govern our lives."[4] The power of ideas and ideals in the formation of decisions and actions concerns character and requires education and wisdom.

The concept of wisdom seems to have disappeared in school and in discussions about education. However, the ability to make wise choices is what parents want for their children to be able to do as they grow into maturity. In essence, wisdom is evident in decisions if they are congruent with the virtues of justice, fortitude, love, optimism, integrity, gratitude, and humility. Wisdom concerns "right" conduct in relation to others and to oneself.

All of this requires thought and reflection, ideals and ideas, thinking and feeling, compassion and understanding, and solitude and presence. Children must realize that while they gain things, they also must, at times, let go in order to grow and find significance.

Good judgment based on virtues directs when and how to act and how to establish priorities that enable individuals to face provocations and rise above difficulty. Character implies that "you, like all human beings, had the capacity to determine who you are and what you want to be—or should be—over and above what you are by nature. What you are in your essence is an inescapable ethical dimension. You have to choose to be good. In sum, when it comes to the kind of person you are, you and you alone ultimately determine your destiny."[5]

THE LARGER CONTEXT

Today, the focus in children's education is on preparedness for college and career. Current conversations about schools generally revolve around assessment and other metrics to quantify students' levels of preparedness for a high school diploma, admittance into college, and ultimately a job. However, this focus is shortsighted and limiting, and it defies larger conditions that are important.

Life has a deeper purpose than being employed, which is just one of the roles individuals play in life. Employment is a significant part of life, but a well-educated person has a depth of understanding and perspective, as well as the ability to learn new skills. While skills are necessary, they change and must be learned and cultivated consistently over time.

The largest concern is that change is pervasive, and its nature and impact are unknown and speculative. In a sense, considering education as preparation for employment is quite myopic because it is not known which jobs or corporations will be in existence twenty, thirty, or forty years from now when today's school children will be employed.

Technology certainly will have an impact: robotics, gene research, artificial intelligence, biotechnology, and other advancements will alter employment and society. If clear information is not available concerning the economic and employment changes and reforms in the future, how can schools educate and train people for unknown and undefined jobs? Education must provide the values, principles, thinking, and academic content and skills so individuals can transform their abilities and perspectives according to the changing conditions they will face throughout their lives.

Speculation exists about the general types of roles people will play in the workforce in fifteen-plus years. The Rand Corporation research brief stipulated:

> Employees will work in more decentralized, specialized firms; slower labor growth will encourage employees to recruit groups with relatively low labor force participation; greater emphasis will be placed on retraining and lifelong learning; and future productivity growth will support higher wages and may affect the wage distribution. Given this, some policies need to be reexamined.[6]

The Pew Research Center indicates that while automation has thus far impacted mostly blue-collar roles, the coming trend and innovation will threaten to upend white-collar work. Some highly skilled workers will be well rewarded economically, but others will be displaced into lower-level service jobs. In this possible milieu, choices—both policy and personal—must be made.[7]

People in manual service jobs are especially concerned about future employment because of automation. People in government, education, and nonprofits are more optimistic about their jobs in the future.

Rand perceives a shift in importance to knowledge-based work that favors "non-routine, cognitive skills" such as abstract reasoning, problem solving, collaboration, and communication. Education will become a lifelong process to address the change in work, society, and responsibilities.

On another scale, social and political issues will remain complicated, if not more so, in the future. The collision of values, the interpretation of principles, and the changing world and environment will require individuals to analyze and assess issues to ensure concepts of justice, freedom, and citizenship are preserved and prosper. Scientific, technological, and social changes will either be a uniting or a dividing factor in the country. Conflicts will occur. The citizenry must be well-versed in ethics and moral principles and their application.

WHAT IS AN EDUCATED PERSON?

The nation stands on the individual's right to pursue happiness. Public education exists so each individual has the ability and perspective to engage in that pursuit. Active participation is essential; standing silent and expecting to find happiness is not going to bring a life of significance and well-being.

Happiness is not simply predicated on the accumulation of wealth and material things or fame and celebrity. "Happiness is an inner feeling of satisfaction about my life 'as a whole.' The good feeling comes from when I use my talents to make a contribution to something larger than myself—my family, my corporation, my nation—which should, in return treat me fairly."[8]

Happiness, in other words, is using knowledge and talent constructively and responding conscientiously with strong character to the opportunities and challenges of life. If actions are contrary to personal beliefs, then individuals will not be fulfilled regardless of their economic standing or status. Actually, for anyone to find satisfaction, their actions and principles must be aligned—self-interest is not always the goal.

While happiness and meaning are not synonymous, both require more than academic knowledge and content mastery. Ethical understanding, character development, and cultivating wisdom are necessary.

In the United States, we are expected to understand and support the "common good" by protecting the rights of others and holding our government accountable by active citizenship and community involvement. Citizenship is not a passive responsibility. Understanding responsibilities in a democratic society and gaining some sense of historical perspective about duty to family, community, and country are cornerstones to the American way of life nationally and locally.

Today, the explosion of technology and access to information, opinions, and diatribes requires that citizens be well-informed and complex thinkers. Complex thinkers analyze and make distinctions between fact, fiction, opinion, science, and the new concern for "fake news."

To do this, citizens need skeptical and critical thinking skills. Skeptics do not take comments or arguments at face value. They question whether they are true or alleged and therefore challenge them on rational grounds. Skeptics have reservations about the veracity of comments and proposals and the veracity of the undergirding assumptions, facts, or philosophy. Educated people ask questions. They are skeptics, not cynics or lemmings. They are engaged civically and stand on principle. They are self-reflective and personally and socially conscious.

Skeptical thinking leads to critical thinking, which is a deliberative process to analyze and evaluate issues. Skeptics question the plausibility of arguments, and critical thinking skills push the issue to further analysis and evaluation.

Change is the consequence of conflict, creativity, and innovation. Intellectual skills are more than simply literacy and numeracy. They involve: gathering information and organizing it, defining the values that undergird arguments, articulating ideas clearly, formulating new perspectives, and questioning assumptions and theories. Analyzing, synthesizing, and evaluating issues, concepts, and information are vital.

Critical thinkers have the ability to correctly understand the information—to interpret and make sense out of information presented in a variety of forms, whether in charts, writing, or media. Then the information can be analyzed—connecting the components and their veracity and meaning. Reasoning is essential in considering the assumptions behind the arguments and their frame of reference. Concepts and principles are reviewed and analyzed. The skills of analysis, synthesis, and evaluation are part of the process.

Without skeptical and critical thinking, individuals can be duped and misled. Learning today requires more challenging thought and serious review because in many cases the background of online users is unknown and their motives and agenda unclear. Citizens need to seek and challenge the empirical research, if any, behind the claims. Unquestioned acceptance of arguments leads to serious personal or social consequences.

Creative, critical, skeptical thinking, and problem solving result in conceptual understanding of necessary information to define and resolve problems. Problem solving involves a broad perspective across content and a deep understanding of the principles and moral expectations to maintain a civil society.

Children need the capacity to see with new eyes: to open their minds and perceive the world with a fresh perspective. They must be mindful and aware of the integration of issues and ideas. Discovering and exploring ideas is at the core of education.

Everyone has times of doubt and uncertainty. Children need to learn how to reflect and deliberate in these times. They need to experience the satisfaction that comes with using their minds and curiosity to define issues, finding solutions, and standing up for beliefs based on sound analysis and clear argument.

All citizens need to understand the philosophical values and principles because here is the inevitable clash of ideas and interests. Listening, perceiving, and understanding connections in our lives are important to continue to learn and adapt. An ethical understanding of core values and the conflicts they raise is essential for establishing an honorable future, particularly in times of change.

An open mind and heart involves the intersection of understanding our obligations to others and to ourselves. Acting with integrity moves beyond simply reciting knowledge or comprehending data. Empathy, honesty, and compassion are important. Students need the background to analyze, interpret, and determine a course that is credible and in concert with a just, fair, and ethical path and outcome.

In an unfolding world, creativity and continuous intellectual curiosity to respond and shape the future are required. Children must be able to succeed and fail safely, discover their uniqueness, and understand the connections they have to the world, society, and others. A good education helps children discover what wants to emerge from within them: who they are and what their mission and purpose in life is.

The most difficult question we have to answer is: "Who am I?" No standardized test can measure this; although perversely, it can stymie the pursuit. Answering the question "Who am I?" is essential to self-understanding and acting with integrity because it defines the principles on which individuals stand.

Children are searching to discover themselves—their talents, uniqueness, and path in life. Education has a spiritual dimension, not in a religious sense, but by helping children to grasp life's meaning and purpose and developing their mindfulness and consciousness of the world around them as well as their relationship to others and to themselves.

Creativity and beauty are stimulating and uplifting, touching hearts and souls as well as the senses and imagination. People require sustenance for their imaginations and souls, as well as their physical and mental health. Our souls need nourishment from the arts—music, art, theater, and literature—to spur originality, expression, and reflection. The fine arts are basic to emotional, symbolic, and cognitive understanding vital to the development of an educated person.

Education is about living fully with purpose and meaning. Happiness emanates from a life well-lived and comes from each person capitalizing on their uniqueness and following their heart, as well as their intellect, in finding their path in life.

CONSCIOUSNESS AND COURAGE

Basic to life's journey is how children feel about themselves. Self-concept determines whether they feel empowered to decide and act or feel impotent and become passive and benign. Making sense of experiences and events is not always easy. The universe cannot be controlled, but individuals can control how they respond to it. How they feel about themselves is important to their well-being.

Self-concept directs and filters interactions and activities. For example, individuals must learn to be independent of social environment and not to be tied to external rewards and punishments. In essence, they have to find those rewards within themselves. Finding enjoyment and meaning in the ongoing flow of life and experience does not require external rewards.

Children must learn to live "consciously," which is part of being free and autonomous, not dependent on others to make choices for them. "To live consciously means to be open to perceiving the world around and within us, to understand the circumstances, and to decide how to respond to them in ways that honor our needs, values, and goals."[9]

Basically, it means being aware of inner and outer worlds: being self-aware and self-reflective about their thinking and the conclusions they draw. Consciousness highlights sensations, perceptions, feelings, and ideas. Acting consciously requires facing issues and making decisions in harmony with personal values and goals.

This isn't always easy. Sometimes it means standing alone on principle— being the wolf howling in the wilderness with the courage to go against the social or political grain. Courage, however, is not being free of fear. In fact it requires overcoming it by "internalizing the conviction that the goals you are accomplishing are worth risking the penalties you face. Sacrifice is made sensible. Put differently, perseverance, courage, stamina, and determination necessary to overcome the inertia, skepticism and systemic resistance . . . are rooted in the leader's beliefs and depth of conviction."[10]

Examples exist of individuals having to face horrendous circumstances and still able to find meaning in life. Viktor Frankl indicated that we can find meaning in life "by creating a work or doing a deed, by experiencing something or encountering someone, or by the attitude we take toward unavoidable suffering."[11]

Life presents challenges and opportunities. Individuals have to live life even though they do not control much in this world. However, they do determine their attitude and behavior toward circumstances and challenges. People are able. They can act. They are not without virtue. They have an internal life and an external one. They can live consciously and not fall adrift to external social, political, or other forces.

As poet, John O'Donohue wrote:

> Every human heart is full of longing. You long to be happy, to live a meaningful and honest life, to find love, and to be able to open your heart to someone; you long to discover who you are and to learn how to heal your own suffering and become free and compassionate. To be alive is to be suffused with longing. The voices of longing keep your life alert and urgent. If you do not discover the shelter of belonging within your life, you could become a victim and target of your longing, pulled hither and thither without any anchorage anywhere.[12]

POINTS TO REMEMBER

- Education is more than cognitive exercises and standardized testing. It is about self-understanding, thinking, ideas, principles, ethics, beauty, and culture.
- Parents are in widespread agreement about the priorities children should be taught in school: responsibility, hard work, and independence.
- Ethics, values, and character are important in children's development and in their finding purpose, meaning, and commitment.
- Education plays an indispensable role in developing children's character, behavior, and socioemotional development.
- Character defines individuals—who they are is revealed through their words and behavior.
- Autonomy requires individuals to make wise and ethical decisions in the face of difficult circumstances and choices.
- Skeptical and critical thinking are essential to being well-educated.
- Self-concept determines whether children will feel empowered to act or be passive observers in life.

NOTES

1. Mortimer J. Adler, *Reforming Education*, ed. Geraldine van Doren (New York: Macmillan, 1977), 231.
2. Kim Parker, "Families May Differ, but They Share Common Values on Parenting," Pew Research Center, September 18, 2014, http://www.pewresearch.org/fact-tank/2014/09/18/families-may-differ-but-they-share-common-values-on-parenting/.
3. Mike Rose, *Why School?* (New York: The New Press, 2009), 103.
4. Gary Hart, *The Good Fight* (New York: Random House, 1993), 4.
5. Rand Corporation, "The Future at Work—Trends and Implications," 2004, http://www.rand.org/pubs/research_briefs/RB5070/index1.html.
6. Rand Corporation, "The Future at Work."
7. Aaron Smith, "AI, Robotics, and the Future of Jobs," Pew Research Center, August 6, 2014, http://www.pewinternet.org/2014/08/06/future-of-jobs/.
8. William J. O'Brien, *Character at Work* (New York: Paulist Press, 2008), 13.
9. Fred Kofman, *Conscious Business: How to Build Value through Values* (Boulder, CO: Sounds True, 2006), 3.
10. O'Brien, *Character at Work*, 130.
11. Viktor Frankl, *Man's Search for Meaning* (New York: Washington Square Press, 1984), 133.
12. John O'Donohue, *Eternal Echoes* (New York: HarperCollins, 1999), 7.

Chapter Two

Students and Victim Mentality

"Your purpose in life may be to become more who you are and more engaged with the people and the life around you, to really live your life. That may sound obvious, yet many people spend their time avoiding life." —Thomas Moore

Connor walked into the kitchen where his mother was making supper. She turned from the boiling potatoes on the stove and looked at him with concern. He stopped by the sink for a glass of water and looked at her.

"I heard from your English teacher today," she said with a tone of irritation. "She said you are getting a D in her class because you haven't turned in four assignments and are not paying attention. She sent me an e-mail and asked me to give her a call about this."

Connor stood and looked at her for a second. "I thought I turned everything in. She must've lost those assignments. Besides, some of them are really stupid."

"Lost them?"

"Yeah, she isn't organized. She doesn't tell us what's expected and how to do it." He paused. "She just contacted you today? The quarter is almost over! How am I supposed to make everything up that she says I didn't do?"

"Well, I'm not happy. Are you sure you turned them in? When I call her, I have to find out why she didn't notify me sooner. This is awfully late. How can you get all this done now?"

"Yeah. Besides, she doesn't really like me. She plays favorites."

Teachers shake their heads at some of the excuses students make for their performance in school—and why some parents are so willing to accept their stories. Unfortunately, these kinds of narratives occur more frequently today.

Basically, the "It's not my fault" attitude may imply something more serious if it is occurring regularly.

Victim behavior is evident today at home and school and even in the workplace. We hear it in our communication. Listen to young children: "The milk spilled," "The toy broke," or, especially if there are brothers or sisters at home, "He/she made me do it." Young children frequently say these things to avoid discipline over the spilled milk. Did the milk really spill by itself, are there really self-destructing toys, and are siblings always the cause of problems?

But older students' language also betrays an attitude that is geared to deflecting responsibility. How often do we hear: "The class is useless; we don't learn anything!" "My teacher doesn't explain things," "All you do is criticize me," "The coach is always on my back," "No one cares about my feelings," or "The teacher is out of it; nobody likes him." These negative comments are geared to placing the burden on others for their circumstances rather than on themselves.

Generally, these responses carry one of three themes. Each one is a victim story: I am innocent, and it is not my fault for what has happened. The second theme is "It is all your fault": I am innocent at the hands of a villain or perpetrator. Or the third story line: I am helpless and there is nothing I can do to correct the situation. Unfortunately, today it seems that many individuals and groups respond this way. Any individual responsibility for outcomes and events is denied.

OUTLOOK ON LIFE

Individuals with a victim mentality are not optimists. People often perceive pessimists as intellectual realists—the sensible, non-Pollyanna-ish personalities, who see things as they really are and not through so-called rose-colored glasses. Similar to victim mentality, however, pessimism can constrict individuals in an attitude of passive preoccupation, negative expectation, and solemn acceptance.

Voltaire sarcastically stated, "Optimism . . . is a mania for maintaining that all is well when things are going badly." The mindset with this perspective is that there is never a case for optimism because things seldom go the way envisioned or planned. Darkness hovers and looms. Trust is nonexistent.

Optimism or pessimism concerns the expectation for what the future holds. Pessimists and self-victimizers believe things will not work out well—the game is rigged, people are against them, they don't have any advantages, or it will take too much work and effort—and then, of course, there's the fear of failure.

Optimists, on the other hand, believe things can work out well but action is necessary—blaming and whining are not appropriate actions. "Optimism is thus defined as a set of beliefs that leads people to approach the world in an active fashion."[1] Action means decisions and engagement; victim mentality is the exact antithesis.

Optimism involves and influences a person's total being: mind, body, and spirit. It leads to action, which is sometimes difficult and demanding. Effort and involvement, not perching passively on the sidelines, is the attitude. Choices and decisions must be made to create positive outcomes or, when they fall short, to determine the reasons for shortcomings or failures.

"Consider optimism and pessimism as beliefs that developed through the assimilation and accommodation of new information, just as all beliefs do. In some cases, new information is simply fit into someone's habitual view of things. In other cases, it mediates changes from an optimistic view to a pessimistic one, or vice versa."[2] This occurs through each phase of childhood and ongoing development.

Through thoughtful reasoning, meaning becomes clear and provides understanding and peace. Optimists can mindfully learn and accept why things happen and do something about it. Pessimists throw up their arms in dismissive exasperation.

CHILD DEVELOPMENT AND OPTIMISM

As children grow from childhood to adulthood, cognitive development is taking place concerning changes in perception, memory, intelligence, problem solving, and language. In the process, children learn to transform and make sense of information, which becomes more complex because of its availability through a number of varied sources—personal, data, observation, reading, listening, technology. Information has impact, and how it is perceived is dependent, in part, on an individual's frame of mind.

As children move from birth to age six, they are egocentric and see things solely from their own viewpoint. At this stage, they begin demonstrating optimism and pessimism about possible future events and outcomes. They can confuse luck and skill when they explain outcomes and frequently downplay the role of effort and initiative.

From seven to eleven, children think more concretely and logically. Adult-like optimism and pessimism begin to appear at this age. They see how certain actions result in some outcomes but not in others. In this age span, they can work backward from outcomes to understanding the actions that led to them.

At age twelve and older, the final stage of cognitive development begins as children begin to operate in the abstract. Adolescents can think about and examine issues such as justice, friendship, love, self, and life's meaning. They can begin to see the world and their lives as they might be or could be, not just as they presently are.

Optimism and pessimism are extremely relevant because they provide platforms from which to see and examine issues and the world generally. Points of view and perspective develop that may be independent of parents, teachers, and other adults. They look to peers and away from parents for guidance; hence, the choice of peer group can influence their sense of pessimism and optimism.

Optimism and pessimism are focused on the future, and children gain a sense of their ability to respond based on those perspectives. Children, however, are grounded in the present reality: if the present is clouded by capriciousness, chaos, or confusion, then pessimism can become the most likely viewpoint. If the present seems ordered and calm, then children may see things more optimistically. Confronting difficult and negative situations and experiencing successful outcomes nurture optimists, which is the result of several influences.

Children who experience triumphs feel optimistic. Success breeds success because the circumstances vindicate a sense of optimism. Conversely, being proclaimed a loser or failure—by others or through self-proclamation—can cause pessimism to evolve.

People significant to the children have a major influence on their optimistic or pessimistic disposition. Adult feedback to children is important. Feedback reinforcing they have some control and can make a positive effort to deal with the circumstances supports an optimistic viewpoint. Suggesting that the child was inept in getting a positive outcome can lead to pessimism; for example, the lack of intelligence or their socioeconomic status are examples beyond the child's control that can lay a pessimistic foundation.

Adults constantly model behavior, and children adopt the ways of significant adults, mentors, and role models. If children hear and see a hopeful, positive outlook about the future, then they will, too. If pessimism is in play, they will adopt that perspective because it has been modeled for them. Optimistic people remember their parents as happy and active people, with positive self-images. Discovering that a sense of humor is an asset in life also helps. Optimistic parents produce optimistic children.

Optimism is a "social product."[3] Being consistent, positive, and responsive, along with giving children responsibility, encourages their independence and helps them build a sense of confidence. Learning to discriminate between different failures helps develop the capacity to master problem solving and recast failure into a challenge and ultimately a solution.

Not all failures have the same roots. Some occur because of the nature of the circumstances and the ability to make decisions that can directly alter events. Other failures are due to numbness or lack of effort and persistence.

Efforts to master highly difficult and uncontrollable situations are different from failing due to poor attitudes or lack of effort.

Finally, some children experience grave situations or disappointments. The death of a parent or other such losses can push children into a pessimistic or at least a confused mind frame. The age of the child matters here. If the child is mature enough to understand they had no responsibility for the loss, then they can maintain a more optimistic life view. If that is unclear, then they can become at risk for a pessimistic frame of mind. The loss of a parent is a fearful trauma creating uncertainty about the stability of life and the world and the child's relationship to it.

Optimistic children understand emotions, seek more information, try to discover solutions, understand the bright side of events, seek help from other people, and try to analyze why things happen as they do. Pessimists become angry and depressed and blame conditions, fate, or others for their condition and position.

LIFE HAPPENS

Inevitabilities exist in life: it is not a flat line but involves wonderful peaks, complicated valleys, and open plains. The surprising bends, curves, and forks make life's journey interesting and demanding—and sometimes inspiring. However, on the road of life dark times are unavoidable—deaths occur and losses strike. Everyone wants children's pursuit of happiness to be successful and exhilarating and without trouble or pain.

Celebrating life really means accepting its challenges and opportunities and shortcomings and victories. Who would want to be stuck experiencing a "Groundhog Day," à la Bill Murray, living the same day over and over again (although he did make different choices that resulted in different outcomes)?

Life and its unpredictability offer possibilities and tests that inspire and motivate. Difficulties can present new perspectives and insights along with a variety of options. The question is what to do with the alternatives and the choices available and how to deal with complicated situations and personal responsibilities.

Everyone has a choice to either be an active participant or become a victim who rejects responsibility and the freedom to act and meet their responsibilities. Kets de Vries in his research states:

> Bad things happen to all of us; that's life. It's not a rose garden. But there are many different ways of dealing with the difficulties that come our way. Most of us, when faced with life's obstacles, do something about them and get on with it. But people with a victim mentality are incapable of doing so. Their negative outlook on life transforms every setback into a major drama. Even their way of absorbing information causes chaos and stress. To complicate this

already difficult equation, people suffering from the victim syndrome are prone to aggravate the mess in which they find themselves. Strange as it may sound, they are often victims by choice. And ironically, they are frequently successful in finding willing victimizers.[4]

VICTIM MENTALITY

Conversations today are filled with stories of individuals who are always blaming someone else for their state of affairs. People become very frustrated with those individuals and the nonproductive and aggravating drama they create. They can't understand why these individuals are so negative and always complaining.

Self-identified victims use language that carries some common characteristics. They play the "poor me" card and never feel answerable for their situations or behavior. They always expect the worst, and conversations are centered on the unfairness of their problems and the people who are to blame—the implication being that they were not culpable for the situation and were powerless to address it.

Behaving as an impotent victim and avoiding opportunities to help themselves is characteristic of this behavior. They fail to act and they try to avoid difficult circumstances. In some cases, because they have failed before, they feel that they are incapable of improving their present state or performance.

Sometimes in life a correct decision is to do nothing—not to respond. This may be an active and proper choice for the specific context. For individuals with victim mentality, however, doing nothing is a pattern that becomes inappropriately passive-aggressive, causing events to be exacerbated and spiral out of control.

This mentality alters the locus of control from internal to external. They perceive that the locus of control is external—outside of their sphere, not internal and within their influence. Hence, they feel incapable of influencing or managing situations.

Kets de Vries states, "People with a victim mentality display passive-aggressive characteristics when interacting with others. Their behavior has a self-defeating, almost masochistic quality. The victim style becomes a relational mode—a life affirming activity: I am miserable therefore I am."[5]

The upshot of this attitude is giving up, asserting that actions are futile, and believing that they are not able or simply not willing to put forth effort. Finding and assigning culpability to others is characteristic.

Their passive-aggressive position makes them bystanders in life and events. Sitting on the sidelines, they criticize, second-guess, or condemn those who are actively involved. However, they hold themselves blame-free because from their viewpoint they are responsibility-free of any cause or outcome. By doing so, they pay the price of powerlessness and helplessness—but continue to harangue.

Blaming others establishes themselves as victims of external circumstances. Kofman asserts that some victims think playing victim protects their self-esteem and innocence. "We have the ability to respond to our circumstances and influence how they affect us. In contrast, the unconditional blamer defines his victim-identity by his helplessness, disowning any power to manage his life and assigning causality only to that which is beyond his control. Unconditional blamers believe that their problems are always someone else's fault, and that there's nothing they could have done to prevent them."[6]

Passive-aggressive behavior toward others is a means of getting what they want when things unfold poorly. Because they are experienced excuse makers, they get their way by laying "guilt trips" on others by sulking, pouting, withdrawing, excuse making, and lying. Sympathy, and the attention it brings, is the goal.

As adept manipulators, they turn things upside down. Even with the blame game and dour outlook and drama, victims attract people to them because of the altruism others feel to help someone in need. This attraction, however, eventually wears thin because nothing seems to work in helping them. The blaming and refusal to accept responsibility eventually discourages and frustrates helpers and creates a divide.

Ironically, the intent to help provides the attention and affection the self-proclaimed victim may not have gotten otherwise. Pity and sympathy for the victim can create a sense of validation and results in a continuation of that behavior. Shifting a sense of misery onto others may feel cathartic at first, but it is also destructive.

In actuality it may generate more difficult circumstances because the self-victimizer stops any questioning or self-reflection about the issues or their behavior and continues to deflect accountability. They stay stuck in the dysfunctional behavior pattern. Eventually relationships fracture, resulting in greater conflict and isolation.

IMPACT OF VICTIM MENTALITY

Victim mentality is a result of "learned helplessness," which eventually destroys the individual's ability to realize their potential and aspirations. It is disempowering and based on the thinking that external forces control circumstances and that ducking responsibility protects them from the stigma of failure. Failing is not always negative. In fact, a positive self-concept is based, in part, on responding, failing, and overcoming.

Everyone, from time to time, has uncomfortable feelings about their abilities. But excuse making and ducking responsibility prevents the opportunity to learn and improve. Victim mentality pushes them to convince others to cover for them, rather than acting on their own behalf. The net result is that confidence dwindles and reticence increases as any creative effort is focused on diverting responsibility.

Most individuals desire greater freedom and autonomy—particularly teenagers who press against parental and other restrictions. Self-proclaimed victims restrict their own autonomy and, in reality, become dysfunctional in everything but complaining. In adult situations at work or any other social relationships, this attitude is self-destructive. Those caught in victimhood strike out at others to defend their helplessness, creating conflict and divorcing others from them.

Being self-reliant has always been an American maxim. Maturity means confronting and working through tough times, including deaths, natural disasters, failures, physical issues, and victimization from bullies and others. Being paralyzed by self-victimization deters any opportunity for growth and developing maturity. Being entrapped in a victim mentality is incapacitating and corrosive.

In a broader sense, Norman Cousins stated, "The enemy is a man who not only believes in his own helplessness but actually worships it. His main article of faith is that there are mammoth forces at work, which the individual cannot possibly comprehend, much less alter or direct. And so he expends vast energies in attempting to convince other people that there is nothing they can do. He is an enemy because of the proximity of helplessness to hopelessness."[7]

CHOICES

In our society, everyone has the opportunity to make choices, including a choice whether or not to adopt a victim mentality and how to respond to emotions, conditions, and the world around them. Attitudes are in response to feelings and perceptions, as well as to the cognitive information at hand. Certainly intelligence is important, but emotional intelligence (EQ) is, too.

Daniel Goleman identifies key emotional intelligence abilities such as reining in and controlling emotional impulses, being self-motivating, and persisting in the face of frustrations.[8] In addition, he cites other important factors such as the ability to regulate moods to keep distress from squelching thought.

Acting appropriately socially and wisely in human relationships takes more than cognitive excellence. In essence, one can be smart with a high intelligent quotient (IQ) but not wise and not apply it effectively because of low emotional intelligence where decisions become circumvented by emotions.

Choices are available for everyone, and both intellectual and emotional aspects should be considered in making them. Obviously, accountability is part of the decision-making equation—even in failing to decide. In essence, situations present choices and choices elicit cognitive and emotional reactions. That is why both IQ and EQ are important.

Key considerations in making choices are self-awareness and living consciously. "There is not much we as individuals can do to change the way the universe runs. . . . How we feel about ourselves, the joy we get from living, ultimately depend directly on how the mind filters and interprets every day experiences. Whether we are happy depends on inner harmony, not on the controls we are able to exert over the great forces of the universe."[9]

In a similar vein, Kofman stated, "To live consciously means to be open to perceiving the world around us and within us, to understand circumstances, and to decide how to respond to them in ways that honor our needs, values, and goals. To be unconscious is to be asleep, mindless. To live unconsciously means to be driven by instincts and habitual patterns."[10] Being conscious about relationships, issues, surroundings, and their internal selves allows individuals to face circumstances and make decisions that can actually help them and improve conditions.

Playing the victim mentality card basically is insensitive and blind to actively moving ahead and making progress and finding satisfaction. Passive-aggression, and the negative attitudes and nonresponse to the circumstances it embodies, builds neither lasting relationships nor internal or external harmony.

Individuals conscious of the world around them speak the truth and do not lie. They don't compromise values for the sake of sympathy and attention. They find creative solutions and understand their emotions, not disparaging or blaming others for that for which they were responsible.

Unconditional blamers relinquish credibility over time and degrade and eliminate their ability to use their influence and power. While self-defined victims try to hide under a veil of innocence, they eventually lose trustworthiness and authenticity. For children in a social context, this can be severely destructive, just as it is immensely destructive in the adult workplace.

The distinguished psychologist Csikszentmihalyi describes consciousness as a clearinghouse of internal and external information that influences individuals and how they can react.[11] Feelings, perceptions, and ideas help guide priorities. Children and others can act, not as passive victims, but as active individuals who can affect the quality of their lives. Conscious individuals understand that to address the situations and decisions they face, it is necessary to "know thyself."

A WORD ON BULLYING VS. VICTIM MENTALITY

Bullying is a hot topic with parents, schools, and other agencies. Being victimized by a bully occurs in childhood and adulthood and at school or at work or socially.

Victim mentality in this book is an internal state consciously adopted to deflect responsibility and failure. With bullying, however, an external individual or others are the cause of the oppression and hurt. Certainly anyone who is bullied feels a sense of rejection from the aggression and experience.

Three criteria distinguish a bully-victim relationship from other forms of harassment. They include: (1) intentional negative actions or harm doing, (2) actions carried out repeatedly and over a period of time, (3) an imbalance of power, with the bully in a position of greater psychological or physical strength over the victim.[12]

In a bullying situation, abuse can come through emotional, verbal, physical, or cyber events. The purpose is to abuse, intimidate, or dominate others, which can take place in one-on-one situations or through group experiences. Sometimes, bullying is physical—stealing, fighting, or destroying property. Verbal bullying is through name-calling, spreading rumors, verbal threats, or belittling the individual to hurt their reputation or social standing.

Today, students and others experience bullying through the Internet or other technological means. E-mail, text messages, social network sites, cell phones, and other technological devices are used.

Certainly, individuals facing bullying can react in ways that are harmful to them. Some people withdraw socially when confronted with any form of bullying, and some blame themselves for the action of the perpetrators. Depression, anger, acting out, and other approaches are the results of being victimized by others.

Victim mentality, however, is different. It is learned and not inborn or imposed by others, so it is possible for the individual to change it. While those with a victim mentality blame others for a situation that they created themselves or were a significant part of, they do so because they are unwilling to assume any liability for their own actions. They think other people have negative intentions toward them and get short-term pleasure from receiving pity from others from their exaggerated stories they fabricated about the actions of others.

SCHOOLS AND FRAMES OF MIND

Peterson and Bassio indicate that optimists are better students than pessimists.[13] Optimists approach studying and learning differently. They:

- set goals for themselves
- do not rely on externally imposed goals
- perceive themselves as competent
- express limited anxiety during tests
- apply various strategies to learn material
- take a broad view of their own learning: thinking about thinking, problem solving
- think critically and originally
- manage the setting for studying
- seek help from others

In essence, they take charge of their circumstances and demonstrate leadership in their own lives. They set the specific outcomes they desire and move beyond vague goals like "do your best." They have self-efficacy, motivation, and confidence and believe they can achieve the goals. In essence, they are better problem solvers and persevere, continuing to work even in the face of disappointments. In addition, they build positive relationships and do not sever them through negativism and self-pity.

Optimists see choices. They make decisions in an area of life they want to experience and establish goals and seek out other positive people. At times, everyone experiences a sense of optimism or pessimism. These beliefs are not in a vacuum but are related to other views about the world, society, the present, the future, and themselves. These beliefs are interwoven, and each influences the others.

Individuals can seek to find meaning and purpose in traumatic experiences and a chaotic world. They can learn what is important in life and make as much sense of difficult circumstances as they can. They are able to take a philosophical approach to life events, learn lessons, and understand and adapt to setbacks and disappointments. While the world cannot always be changed unilaterally, they are able to continue to be active participants, choose their own path, and have the grit and self-efficacy to take responsibility for their actions.

THE BIGGER PICTURE

Children need to grow into independent and accountable adults if they are to be successful. Becoming responsive and mature people takes strong parenting, good schools, and a deep personal commitment to take control of their lives and continue to learn to be responsible individuals, parents, and citizens. Actually, the American Dream and core ideals rest on a positive sense of the future, confidence, resilience, and personal growth.

In practical life, assuming a victim mentality is a decision for stagnation and complacency and will not achieve growth or progress because it is based on an external locus of control rather than an internal one. As stated earlier, individuals cannot control the universe and every experience they confront, but they do control themselves. There really is no reason not to be able to respond in their best interests.

As John Gardner states, "It does mean recognizing that ultimately you are the one who's responsible for you."[14] The lesson is that children have to learn that they should not engage in self-destructive behavior. That it is their responsibility to learn how to manage circumstances so they don't behave in ways that ensure bad consequences. The "poor me" attitude is a recipe for failure.

Basically, children have to learn they are responsible for their emotions and attitudes and whether they choose a positive or negative outlook about life. It boils down to deciding whether external forces and events will control them or they will take charge of their lives and address those conditions to the best of their ability. This attitude results in learning life's lessons, developing greater maturity, and addressing the challenges that inevitably lay ahead of them. While there is no guarantee of success, the biggest failure is an inability to make responsible choices and decisions.

Victim mentality is a sure way to stymie self-discovery, continued learning, and mature adaptation to life, as well as positive relationships. Facing reality and making choices and decisions requires courage and a strong sense of character, which are essential for children to meet their potential or find purpose and meaning in their individual lives.

POINTS TO REMEMBER

- An individual's outlook on life—optimism or pessimism—directs their perceptions, decisions, and involvement.
- Parents and significant adults influence children's optimistic or pessimistic view of life. Certain events in life also influence a child's optimistic or pessimistic disposition.
- Life presents obstacles, and there are different perspectives and ways of dealing with them.
- Victim mentality is a learned behavior, not imposed by others, and it is possible to change it.
- People with a victim mentality display passive-aggressive characteristics—they give up, assert that actions are futile, and assign blame that is destructive to them and others.

- Individuals with a victim mentality reject the power to manage their lives and adopt and define their identity by helplessness, which is used as a manipulative strategy to get other's sympathy.
- Situations present choices, and making choices not only depends on intelligence but also requires emotional intelligence, self-awareness, and living "consciously."
- "Conscious" individuals understand that to address situations and make decisions they must "know thyself."
- An internal locus of control is important to manage the events and circumstances in life. An external locus of control is characteristic of those with a victim mentality.

NOTES

1. Christopher Peterson and Lisa M. Bassio, *Health and Optimism* (New York: The Free Press, 1991), 9.
2. Ibid., 66.
3. Ibid., 85.
4. Manfred F. R. Kets de Vries, "Are You a Victim of the Victim Syndrome?" faculty and research working paper, INSEAD, 2012, https://sites.insead.edu/facultyresearch/research/doc.cfm?did=50114.
5. Ibid., 3.
6. Fred Kofman, *Conscious Business: How to Build Value through Values* (Boulder, CO: Sounds True, 2006), 18.
7. Norman Cousins, *Human Options* (New York: W.W. Norton and Company, 1981), 61.
8. Daniel Goleman, *Emotional Intelligence* (New York: Bantam, 2005), 34.
9. Mihaly Csikszentmihalyi, *Flow* (New York: HarperCollins, 2008), 9.
10. Kofman, *Conscious Business*, 3.
11. Csikszentmihalyi, *Flow*, 24.
12. Monica J. Harris, *Bullying, Rejection, and Peer Victimization: A Social Cognitive Neuroscience Perspective* (New York: Springer, 2009), Kindle edition, 5.
13. Peterson and Bassio, *Health and Optimism*, 117.
14. John Gardner, *Living, Leading, and the American Dream* (San Francisco: Jossey-Bass, 2003), 45.

Chapter Three

Response-able or Passive Victim?

"You can't be neutral on a moving train." —Howard Zinn

"Passivity may be the easy course, but it is hardly the honorable one." —Noam Chomsky

"In a dependent relationship, the protégé can always control the protector by threatening to collapse." —Barbara W. Tuchman

Vera, an eighth grader, was sent to the principal's office out of her first period math class. She was an average student, and her mother and father ran a business downtown.
   "Why are you here?" the principal asked. Vera looked at her silently. "Well, why are you in my office this morning?" Vera sat quietly again, not responding, looking irritated. "Okay, sit here, I'll be back," the principal said as she walked to the door. She turned and said, "When I return—we will talk."
   Fifteen minutes went by and the principal returned and sat down in front of her. "Vera, why were you sent to the office?"
   Vera looked at her and said, "You know."
   "I want you to tell me. What happened that Mrs. Zanzal sent you to the office?"
   "She said I talked back to her."
   "Talked back? What does that mean?"
   "I don't know. . . . She's always on my case."
   The principal sat quietly for a couple of minutes and looked at her. "On your case?"
   "Yeah, she . . . she's impatient."
   "How so?"

"Other kids say she's a . . . a . . . crabby . . ."

" . . . So why are you here, Vera? You're here because your teacher is crabby? What's up?"

"She knew I wasn't feeling well and she kept asking me how to solve a math problem. She should have known I didn't feel good. But no! She kept on my case."

"So?"

Vera looked down and then abruptly looked up at the principal. "I called her a bitch!"

"So that's why you're here!"

"Yes."

The principal leaned forward and said quietly. "Okay, so what are you going to do about this?"

"What? Me? What am I going to do?"

"Yes, that's right. What are you going to do now?"

"I don't know. I don't care. Just suspend me. . . . Suspend me from school. That's what you're supposed to do, isn't it?"

"No, Vera. You have the problem with Mrs. Zanzal. How are you going to solve this?

"I don't know. . . . Just suspend me. You're in charge of discipline, and anyway I don't think she wants me back in class."

"No, Vera. You got yourself into this situation. How are you—how should you get yourself out of it? You created the situation; now you have to solve it. You have to respond to the situation—not me. You created it; you have to solve it."

Vera's behavior was totally inappropriate and disrespectful to Mrs. Zanzal. But she didn't want to be held responsible for examining her behavior with her teacher or for solving her problem. Getting suspended from school would have given her another arrow for her victim quiver.

Children need to reflect on their behavior and issues and solve things when they go wrong. For some kids, a suspension is just a vacation from school and another reason why other people are the cause of their problems. Having to confront the issue with a teacher and find a respectful solution is far more difficult than a couple of days of suspension from school.

Children don't always realize that every response they make is a choice, including doing nothing and behaving as a victim. Victims perceive everything from a negative lens—"not my fault," "I'm done with it—you decide."

Being a victim is often based on the perception that everything that happens is due to other people's actions and behavior. This attitude results in convincing themselves that they do not have to consider any responsibility for their situations, which gives them permission to not seek a solution. It happened and they want to walk away from it or look for someone to rescue them, which keeps them dependent and passive.

Most people, by nature, have a perception of how things are supposed to evolve and work out. Complaining when they don't or withdrawing into a shell is counterproductive. Things do not always go as planned or desired, but frustration and impotence to respond are destructive and sidesteps any responsibility for what occurred, in addition to failing to solve the issue.

Not responding is a form of passive-aggression, which is an unusual phrase.[1] It sounds like an oxymoron because it combines two words—passive and aggression—into an irritating and destructive behavior. This behavior indirectly expresses negative feelings and anger without openly addressing them and places people in uncomfortable or frustrating positions. People get emotionally overwhelmed and relapse into active- or passive-aggressive modes. While passive-aggression may provide short-term respite, it usually creates long-term distress.

Passive-aggressive individuals basically self-sabotage themselves, dooming themselves to failure. The passive-aggressive approach is often based on lack of self-esteem and carries with it complaining, criticizing, and exaggerated claims of misfortune, along with resentful comments about other individuals. Procrastination, inefficiency, impatience, and stubbornness are some of the characteristics of passive-aggressive individuals.

RESPONSIBILITY

Contrary to passive-aggression is assuming and acting responsibly, which has a different perspective and motivation. Responsibility is emblematic of true personal power. The motivation comes from a positive well and is driven by the desire to make things a little better. The underlying principles for responsibility include appreciation, improvement, compassion, connection, and protection of people, mission, commitments, and self-respect. Taking responsibility means putting oneself on the line openly and forthrightly—and, yes, criticism can follow. Meeting responsibilities is a prerequisite for honestly fulfilling obligations and commitments.

Complacency and self-victimization are not involved in meeting responsibilities—they are not part of the equation. Self-efficacy—the belief that individuals expect that they can accomplish things because of their abilities and experience—is at the essence of being responsible. These individuals examine the preferred outcome and then decide on a positive course of action. Coaches or mentors are helpful, as well as individuals who offer positive challenges and support.

Chapter 3
RESPONSE-ABLE

Life is a spectator sport for those with a victim mentality who sit on the sidelines above the fray commenting and criticizing. In reality, however, everyone has responsibilities, as adults, citizens, employees, neighbors, and parents.

Children also have responsibilities in the family and classroom that increase with age and maturity. Responsibilities start with relatively minor demands: behaving when out to dinner, cleaning their bedroom, taking care of siblings. School presents corollary responsibilities about decorum, relationships, and schoolwork.

Maturity raises the ante and responsibilities. Decisions have larger impact and affect more people, and the depth of the impact is more serious, involving matters of ethics and principles. Standing silent may be an appropriate choice at times, but it also may have grave consequences. Obligations and values may be involved that require dedication.

Obligations are of a higher standard than responsibilities. There are moral overtones to obligations, and the commitment is greater. In a sense, people can fulfill responsibilities in a job and still not complete their work and obligations. In searching for meaning and integrity in life, the primary obligation is to people and relationships based on moral principles.

Responsibility requires competence, understanding, judgment, and accountability. Integrity is a key principle and determines the internal strength and external competence of individuals. Playing egocentric or ethically sidestepping games is not acting with honesty or courage: half-truths, avoidance, and misdirection are deceptive and destructive.

Responsible people have the freedom to make decisions and choices. Obviously, this freedom expands with age and is an essential aspect of leading independent and empowered lives. Autonomy and freedom go hand in hand and are pillars of democracy and self-directed lives.

Autonomous adults pursue happiness within the confines of legal and moral guides. Autonomous comes from the Greek word *autonomos*, which means the ability to act independently and having the freedom to do so: self-determination, independence, and self-sufficiency. Autonomy provides the rationale for being able, as individuals, to respond to circumstances in all aspects of their lives.

Kofman uses the term "response-ability":[2] the ability to respond to circumstances. Individuals are responsible for confronting circumstances, even if they are *not* responsible for creating them. In actuality, response-ability empowers individuals to influence circumstances and to do so with integrity to values and principles. Individuals can focus on the aspects of the situation they can influence or direct.

No matter how difficult things seem, it is important for individuals to express their truth in confronting the challenge. While not always responsible for circumstances, they are "response-able" to face them. They have the power and the integrity to influence the situation in accord with their values: the ability to exercise free will and autonomy and choose why and how to respond.

Response-ability is self-empowering, allowing individuals to address issues in their life, whether or not they have direct control. Sometimes circumstances are beyond direct management, but they do control their reactions and feelings—and their response. In that lies their source of power and the ability to act in line with their standards.

Being able to respond does not guarantee success. The cavalry does not gallop over the hill to save the day. Responses may not get the desired outcomes or work out well because they may be untimely, poorly implemented, or not formidable enough to influence the context or situation. Failure happens even if individuals act in a forthright and competent manner. In many cases, it isn't always circumstances beyond control that created the situations or conflict. The cause may have been the action or inaction of the individual.

Proactive people do not wait for things to happen but analyze; determine prospects, forces, and possibilities; and figure out what things can be influenced and addressed. Too often individuals say, "There was nothing I could do about it." Avoiding any attempt to self-examine their behavior and resorting to being victims of conditions or events is not always accurate or factual.

A car crash might not be expected, but driving thoughtfully and putting cell phones down is a proactive act. The loss of a job can be debilitating emotionally and even physically. But acting competently to leave the position with respect and dignity is an option.

Decisions are never always correct or on target. Faulty knowledge, poor analysis, or conflict with principles and values generate problems. In these cases, the autonomy to decide and act demands accountability for choices and decisions.

Responsibility and response-ability require acknowledgment of a personal role in the issue. "Accepting your freedom requires that you account for choices. Freedom and accountability are two sides of the same coin. . . . If you own your actions, you can be asked for your reasons and held accountable for the consequences. Power is the prize of accountability; accountability is its price."[3]

Mindfulness also means being reflective and adapting to conditions and situations. Mature individuals are conscious of outcomes—both subtle and obvious. They analyze their approach, beliefs, and decisions and take action. Being able to be proactive is important, but falling short or failing can create stress and, in some cases, trauma.

Being responsible and response-able and acting with compassion and caring involve living up to obligations and are signs of character and moral fiber. Developing positive character traits is a process that takes thought and reflection, as well as guidance. There are times at home or in school when children have to think about the responsibilities and attitudes that affect their credibility, integrity, relationships, and ultimately effectiveness in pursuing their aspirations and goals.

In discussions with children, they should consider several questions when it comes to their responsibilities.[4]

- What are your responsibilities at home and school?
- What responsibilities will you have to assume when you get older?
- How do you hold others responsible for their behavior?
- How do you hold yourself accountable for your behavior?

These questions can elicit discussions about the congruence of their behavior with expectations and responsibilities. Beginning to examine their behavior against a palette of responsibilities can evolve into reviewing issues of credibility and integrity as well as trust and autonomy.

Parents have a duty to raise children into adulthood with strong and positive character. Parents must realize that they are raising future adults, so they have to take the long view looking into the future. Character is constantly reflected in behavior. Informing and holding children accountable is essential so that when they do confront issues, their tendency will be to act honorably.

At times, parents desire to be friends with their children and are permissive. Other parents can act like autocratic dictators. In both cases, such parenting styles have negative repercussions for children in school and in their relationships.

Authoritative parents, however, are able to combine reasoning, fairness, and love.[5] They provide reasons for their responses, use power to enforce rules if necessary, set standards and expectations for behavior, and do not base decisions solely on a child's desires. These parents have a zero-tolerance policy for disrespectful speech and behavior.

As stated earlier, parents are teaching by example. Treating children with love and respect, as well as demonstrating love and respect to others, is important. With today's technology, children are exposed to behavioral examples that are cruel, profane, narcissistic, and ethically and morally questionable.

Managing a family or school with positive principles and standards is fundamental and essential. Explaining moral objections and making clear the reasons for doing so help children see reasoning based on principles and values. Moral and ethical standards are extremely important in today's society and into the future—children need these principles to guide them in uncertain or changing waters.

Individuals with character use good judgment. In making choices and decisions, there are some guideposts or tests that children should consider. Children should ask themselves the following questions:[6]

- Would I want people to do this to me?
- Would I like it if everyone else did this?
- Does this action represent the whole truth and nothing but the truth?
- How would my parents feel if they found out I did this?
- Does this go against my conscience—will I feel guilty afterward?
- What are the consequences if I do this—to relationships, to respect, and to the future?
- How would I feel if my action was reported on the front page of the local newspaper?

Being responsible involves decisions and decisions have consequences. Children must learn to examine and consider options and think through the possible consequences. In addition, with most decisions, values are involved. Children should ask: What are they and how do they affect others and me? Seeking advice when things are unclear and confusing is a mature thing to do. These steps can alleviate anxiety and stress when having to make important decisions.

Teachers and parents must discipline children and set expectations and hold children responsible for them by not accepting excuses or diversions. Discipline directs children to do what is right and motivates them to do better. Consequences should show them the seriousness of their behavior. They should be able, at certain ages, to define appropriate discipline for their actions.

Teachers and parents have teachable moments that guide children's thinking and form their character. Both are caregivers and have the opportunity to form learning and family communities, operating under knowledge, ethics, standards, and moral obligations.

Children also need the opportunity to serve in leadership roles—in the family, in school, and in the community. Obviously, leadership brings responsibilities. Having to meet them in a designated role can help children see that they are capable of responding to situations in line with those expectations, as well as accepting accountability that is essential in leadership.

POINTS TO REMEMBER

- Every response is a choice, whether it is active or passive.

- Passive-aggressive behavior expresses negative feelings and anger without specifying them directly. It is frequently based on lack of self-esteem.
- Responsibility is emblematic of true personal power based on the desire to make things better.
- Response-ability is the ability to respond to all circumstances, whether they are positive or negative. The basic premise is that individuals have the power and integrity to influence conditions and events.
- Parents should review with their children their responsibilities at home and at school to help them make choices and decisions by using good judgment.

NOTES

1. Jody E. Long, Nicholas J. Long, and Signe Whitson, *The Angry Smile: The Psychology of Passive-Aggressive Behavior in Families, Schools, and Workplaces* (Austin, TX: PRO-ED, 2008), 12.

2. Fred Kofman, *Conscious Business: How to Build Value through Values* (Boulder, CO: Sounds True, 2006), Kindle edition, 31–32.

3. Ibid., 48.

4. Ayner Pala, "The Need for Character Education," *International Journal of Social Sciences and Humanity Studies* 3, no. 2, (2011).

5. Thomas Lickona, *Character Matters* (New York: Touchstone, 2004), 35–59.

6. Ibid., 37.

Chapter Four

Victim Mentality and Life

"It is impossible to live without failing at something, unless you live so cautiously that you might as well not have lived at all—in which case, you fail by default." —J. K. Rowling

"Everybody needs an inner belief that you are in some sense meant to be here, that you can leave the world a little different in a small way." —Charles Handy

Victim mentality is a learned behavior and a destructive one. Costs are high on a number of fronts. Certainly, individuals assuming a victim mentality pay a huge price, but so do family members, friends, coworkers, and society in general.

For the individuals, there may be short-term comfort from shirking accountability. They are off the hook for circumstances and work to elicit sympathy from friends and others for their plight. Sympathy can be consoling in the short-term, but in the long-term, it is cancerous on all levels of relationships and life.

In a curious way, they accrue power and gain attention by spinning the story of their happenings. In these situations, people are less compelled to criticize or upset them. This form of exploitation garners recognition without responsibility but short-circuits their future.

The short-term comfort soon vanishes. The "poor me" pattern grows old. Soon people find it aggravating. They see through the manipulation. Eventually, individuals with victim mentality must stop the anger, self-doubt, and fear if they are to be independent and construct a life of significance. They must confront their pessimistic and destructive outlook on life and liberate themselves from those shackles. They have to become self-aware of what is happening within and outside of themselves.

The price those with victim mentality pay covers a broad spectrum in personal and work-related relationships. Victim mentality does not result in deep friendships or productive work and professional associations. In fact, victim qualities are almost diametrically opposed to what is required in successful family, community, or work connections.

Friendships are at risk. Honesty, loyalty, self-respect, compassion, forgiveness, and self-confidence are the desired qualities in friends. Negativism and the lack of humor do not make for a relationship that is sharing and open. Individuals who attained life satisfaction identified friendships and close relationships as being at their core.

Individuals seek ambition and sociability, emotional maturity and stability, dependability and empathy in a partner or spouse. They want to share their lives with independent and resourceful people, not those who are negative and passive-aggressive.

The scorecard for quality employees is also contrary to those with victim mentality. A strong work ethic along with dependability, positive attitude, self-motivation, flexibility, and the ability to collaborate are what employers desire. Confident, intelligent, and upbeat people outshine dour blamers who poison the work climate and culture with their attitude.

At work, individuals with victim mentality castigate others for their own issues and problems. They act as innocents who have to deal with the stupidity and maliciousness of others. Other people are always the cause of failures and shortcomings, and, of course, they feel there is nothing they can do to prevent or remediate situations or problems.

Employers want individuals to take unconditional responsibility and act to shape circumstances and respond affirmatively to results.[1] On this level, those with victim mentality do not measure up.

On a broader scale, those with victim mentality not only curtail their own life and potential, but their loss may have a broader scope. Losing individual talent and promise is a huge loss for families and possibly for society. Philosophically and practically, when individuals "turtle"—go inside their shell—they eliminate any possibilities they may bring to their relationships. Not getting involved, the inability to share their skills and aptitudes, and engaging in negativism eliminate them from contributing and being a serious resource or factor. Individually, they lose positive connections and purpose, and society loses potential and a unique perspective and ideas that can open doors.

Living in a victim mentality shell handicaps them from truly finding meaning and happiness. A negative mindset and external locus of control result in ineptness, low self-esteem, and a lifetime sentence of anger, frustration, and dissatisfaction. Being a passive-aggressive victim takes an individual out of the game, along with their talent and potential.

WHAT IS HAPPINESS AND MEANING?

Actually, happiness is not hidden, waiting to be found; it takes effort and energy to attain. The impression is not only that the journey itself will bring happiness but also that it is synonymous with finding meaning. Happiness and meaning, however, are not exactly interchangeable. The focus of each is different.

Happiness is more concerned with having needs met: financial security or desired material things. In many ways, it is about having and satisfying personal desires. Money and physical comforts can bring temporary happiness, but they can also leave a void because fiscal resources cannot buy significance or consequence in life.

Meaning is deeper and more internal than materialism and status. Meaning is actually essential to confront life with its peaks and valleys. Personal identity, being able to have a voice, and consciously understanding and interpreting life's experiences pertain to meaning.

Self-knowledge is integral to finding meaning because individuals discover their own path and do not succumb to fads or external pressure to conform. A first step in finding meaning is to "know thyself"—personal intelligence, understanding one's limitations, and perceptiveness about relationships and the views of others.

Kaufman identifies the factors in life related to happiness, meaning, or both.[2] Feeling connected to others and being active and productive contributes to both happiness and meaning.

The factors related to happiness but not meaning, on the other hand, include: finding life easy and not difficult, feeling healthy, taking more from life than giving, and having money and material goods.

On the other side, factors related to meaning but not happiness include: relationships with others, helping people, activities associated with core values, and engaging in creative and thought-provoking ventures.

According to Kaufman, meaning has two major components: cognitive processing and purpose. Cognitive processing concerns making sense of circumstances and integrating experiences. Purpose is more motivational and involves pursuing long-term goals that highlight one's self-identity. Both cognitive processing and purpose require perseverance and grit.

Character is related to finding meaning and happiness because it has to do with how individuals address life. Virtues such as honesty, justice, courage, and compassion are some of the major foundations for how life is lived. They concern conscience and honor and the choices individuals confront and make.

Virtues actually define who people are—to themselves and to others. They define each person through their individual decisions and behavior—concern for the common good, the nature of their relationships, and their involvement in the community and society. Living in ways that are trustworthy, honest, courageous, and compassionate promotes satisfaction and well-being[3] —all byproducts of living with virtue and wisdom.

Meaning in life is found in a challenging and consequential goal that has notable purpose. Carrying through and striving for constructive goals through directed effort is satisfying. From another perspective, setting goals, obtaining skills, getting feedback, and becoming involved can lead to happiness, even in difficult and turbulent times, if individuals are in "control of the mind" and not emotionally disjointed.

"Creating meaning involves bringing order to the contents of the mind by integrating one's actions into a unified flow experience."[4] Someone who knows his desires and works with purpose to achieve them is a person whose feelings, thoughts, and actions are congruent with one another and is therefore a person who has achieved inner harmony. Congruence exists between values and behavior and eliminates any dissonance about how life is lived.

In discussions of meaning, values and philosophy are indispensable. Values and an ethical framework move beyond lower-level needs in Maslow's hierarchy of need framework. Each individual must meet lower-level needs of safety and security first in order to pursue meaning. Self-actualizing, however, involves higher needs of esteem, which involves a sense of accomplishment and achieving one's potential and creative desires.

Extreme circumstances exist in the world today and historically that would seem to curtail any prospect of finding meaning. Viktor Frankl in September 1942 was transported along with his wife and parents to a Nazi concentration camp. His wife and parents died in the camp, but Frankl survived.

After three years in the concentration camp, Frankl and others were liberated. He was a psychologist and neurologist and wrote about the experience in his acclaimed book, *Man's Search for Meaning*. He asserts that the difference between the survivors and those who died was meaning. Finding meaning—having something to live for—made the prisoners more resilient by turning tragedy into personal triumph.

Individuals, he affirmed, have spiritual freedom, which is very significant. Strong forces exist beyond an individual's direct control except one thing: the freedom to choose how to respond to those circumstances. That is solely an individual choice, even in the extreme victimization of the concentration camps. Frankl still had unilateral control over his reactions and actions.

The choice, though small by comparison to the larger social and suppressive political powers, was still his. He chose to control his behavior both spiritually and mentally—he alone controlled his thoughts and attitude.

In a philosophical light, believing that even in brutal circumstances there is more to expect in life provides hope that there is something to live for. In

Frankl's case, it was his book. Those who thought life was hopeless did not expect anything in the future and rejected that there was any reason to live. Knowing the "why" for life can furnish the reason and responsibility to go on living and overcoming horrendous and inhuman conditions.

Today, some adults and children assume a victim mentality in response to issues that are ridiculously minor compared to Frankl's. While he still had the freedom of choice, it was much more limited than most people have in their social, work, or family contexts. He believed that meaning could be created by work or "doing a deed," by experiencing something or meeting someone, or by the attitude we take when we have to face unavoidable suffering.[5]

Identifying purpose in life is an obvious way to pursue meaning. Teachers commit themselves to helping children. Police officers serve their communities at personal risk. Creative artists pursue their art out of the well of personal perspective and creativity. Other professionals are called to their work to find meaning by helping others and fulfilling social values and ethics.

Another way to discover meaning is through experience. For schools, this should actually be one of their main missions. Caring for children and demonstrating love and confidence in them can help them discover who they are, what they believe, and what they are passionate about. Seeing beauty, encountering goodness, and experiencing truth and integrity can open their eyes, as well as the doors of the future.

Human beings and their influence light the candle of meaning and commitment. From these experiences, children, in particular, begin to see positive models and potential selves and to understand how to traverse a changing and sometimes contrary world.

Frankl did not believe that suffering was necessary to find meaning. However, when faced with tragedy or hardship, individuals are able to address such events the best they can and transform them into personal achievements. Standing on principles and values or committing oneself to a cause to stop or protect others from tragedy are examples of suffering being turned into meaning. Facing events, choosing one's attitude, and surviving and learning demonstrate that meaning can be achieved or experienced even in difficulty and adversity.

Meaning is essential: it connects the past to the present to the future. Status, titles, and wealth cannot substitute for the meaning found in ideas, creativity, human connections, integrity, and challenge. In fact, children must learn that we develop character "more through our sufferings then our successes, that setbacks can make us stronger if we don't give in to feeling sorry for ourselves."[6]

Failure has an upside. The bumps along the road can provide the insight and experience that catapults people to success. There are lessons to be learned.

J. K. Rowling, the author of the Harry Potter series, was an unemployed single parent on welfare. Success was a real journey filled with hardships and difficulty. In 2008, she gave a graduation speech at Harvard University, in which she discussed the benefits of failure. Failing is not fun and can be arduous and painful. But it also can be enlightening.

Rowling stated, "So why do I talk about the benefits of failure? Simply because failure meant a stripping away of the inessential. I stopped pretending to myself that I was anything other than what I was, and began to direct all my energy into finishing the only work that mattered to me. Had I really succeeded at anything else, I might never have found the determination to succeed in the one area I believe I truly belonged. I was set free, because my greatest fear had been realized, and I was still alive."[7]

Rowling discovered who she was, why she was here, and where she belonged. In essence, failure can produce wisdom and provide a sense of security by surviving difficult times. Adversity tests many things—resolve, relationships, and a sense of self—and it also can nurture humility and willpower. Resilience and determination are the products, and both are very powerful personal traits.

FINDING THE PATH

Speaking with high school juniors or seniors highlights the pressure some feel about their imminent future after graduation. College? Travel? Employment? Training? They realize that they will move into a new era of autonomy and choice about what their path will be.

Many feel pressure from their parents about what they should do. Certainly, the aspirations their parents have for them and their future can weigh on their minds. Of course, parents look at college from a career and employment angle, hoping for great professional success.

If a four-year college is not in the picture, some students are directed toward technical or trade school—again with the goal of steady and consistent employment. Some examine the military as an alternative, indicating that traveling the world interests them before more education or career considerations bite into their financial future.

All of these discussions have a similar core—"What am I going to do? What do I want my life to be in the future?" Big decisions. Important ones. Potentially, and certainly life-changing ones, as childhood dreams like playing professional hockey for the Chicago Blackhawks or becoming a rock star fade from reality.

The pragmatism of basic security and fiscal needs seems to rule. Many parents, as well as the media, view education through an economic lens, not about living a full and satisfying life complete with purpose and meaning. Self-actualization is not on the radar in these conversations because many feel that it will take care of itself if economic security is at hand.

A consultant was talking to a group of high school students in a wealthy suburb. He asked them what they were going to do after their senior year. One girl stated, "I have to get into Dartmouth."

The consultant asked, "You have to get into Dartmouth? What if you don't, but you get accepted to the University of Michigan?"

She looked at him shocked and said very deliberately, "That . . . would . . . be . . . an . . . absolute . . . disaster."

"But Michigan is a great university."

"I don't care. I must go to Dartmouth. . . . My parents expect it."

Fulfilling expectations of others is very different from following aspirations and ambitions—and meaning.

Philosophy and finding purpose often clash with pragmatism. The question is raised when a student said, "I really want to be a writer. . . . A journalist maybe. But my mom wants me to be a lawyer. She says there are hundreds of unemployed writers and actors serving tea and crumpets in New York. The arts are fine for a hobby. Go to law school!"

In fact, some dread the fact that high school is going to end and that they have choices to make. Some fear independence and autonomy. Many delay decisions, letting options become more limited as the clock ticks closer to graduation.

Conversations like this are stressful for young people. Individuals with a victim mentality do not even try because they don't want to risk failure or they feel they are not capable enough to succeed. Some make a choice about their future and then blame parents, teachers, or others if it doesn't work out. Pessimism dominates and fear rises. Either way, philosophically or pragmatically, they assert that they can sit on the shelf and are not responsible for the outcomes.

Frankl states, "Our industrial society is out to satisfy each and every need, and our consumer society even creates some needs in order to satisfy them. The most important need, however, the basic need for meaning, remains—more often than not—ignored and neglected. And it is so 'important' because once a man's will to meaning is fulfilled, he becomes able and capable of suffering, of coping with frustrations and tensions."[8] Jobs and security are important, but finding meaning and happiness involves more because each person must do what is specifically purposeful to them.

As life goes on, individuals review their choices and decisions, examining what each brought to family, community, and society. What was it that drove them, and did they live a life that was true to themselves, not to what others wanted them to do? Living to please others is hollow, and as Joseph Campbell states, "You are not on your own path if you follow someone else's way. You are not going to realize your potential."[9]

Meaning, as stated earlier, is a major factor in well-being. Living each day and finding significance is important. A seventy-five-year-old person sitting on the front porch doesn't want to review with regret the passion that wasn't followed and lament "what-ifs" and lost chances. After all, everyone has but one life to live. To paraphrase Mark Twain, we will be more disappointed by the things we didn't do than by the things we did do. Failures are a part of everyone's history, but not being true to oneself causes deep regret and sorrow. That is much more difficult to live with than experiencing failure.

Too often children and adults are held back because of their fears or other people's opinions and impressions of them. Contemporary society is filled with distractions and media "noise" that takes them away from internal examination and discovering themselves. People must learn what is within them and who they really are.

Many people think they do not have any special abilities. They focus on their limitations. Everyone has passion and aptitudes, but some are held back by fear of failure or looking stupid or silly. Many teachers see potential and talent in children that the children themselves do not see.

Basically, schools and parents should help children explore and challenge the destructive or limiting notions they have of themselves. Such attitudes and beliefs are constraining and limiting. An open mind is a powerful force in taking a chance and risking falling short. After all, everyone can learn and grow from failure as well as success, but nothing is discovered by not venturing out and exploring yearnings.

The theory behind finding meaning is the ability for each person to use their uniqueness and create their own life. Others cannot do it for them. Creativity cannot be measured through metrically driven examinations. Success comes from getting involved—by hard work and learning from mistakes. Our schools and sometimes families and society do not understand that defeat may have an upside that produces understanding and wisdom.

Finding a mission is exciting and invigorating. When people are involved in something purposeful to them, time moves and passes quickly—being in a state of flow as Csikszentmihalyi wrote: "The concept of flow—the state in which people are so involved in an activity nothing else seems to matter; the experience itself is so enjoyable that people will do it even at great cost, for the sheer sake of doing it."[10]

In this situation, thoughts, feelings, and intention are in harmony and focused on the same goal. Flow is a state where individuals are completely absorbed in what they are doing—fully focused and immersed.

Meaning and purpose are not without struggle. Apples of meaning do not fall from the proverbial tree. Sometimes meaning comes from serendipitous meetings or experiences with people. Difficult events and even suffering bring focus to bear on individuals' inner and outer lives. Introspection is necessary to adapt and to expose and comprehend unknown feelings and perspectives. In some circumstances, meaning is focused on noble goals and values and defines commitment and purpose.

Meaning and happiness together make lives fulfilling. Each individual must find out what lies within them, but not without the risk of stepping out in their own cadence, timing, and direction.

VICTIM MENTALITY AND MATURITY

Victim mentality can be traced back to childhood. Through the influence of parents and others, it is taught by example. When children are very young, parents do not always realize that their son or daughter is learning through observation, even before they can communicate verbally. They watch, and when they are at the age when they can communicate verbally, they listen to and comprehend talk. Children certainly begin to understand emotions through the actions, tone of voice, and comments of parents and other adults.

From all of this, children begin to compose an impression and attitude about life. Along with their own experiences as they grow, children formulate their feelings and react to events. They emulate their parents, family members, or other significant people.

As they move through childhood into adolescence, they adopt a positive or negative perspective of life. Optimistic versus pessimistic views rest on a key issue: whether the conditions in which they interact can or cannot be changed.

Optimists believe circumstances can be changed. Failure can be mediated into success through learning and reflection. Pessimists, on the other hand, assume there is nothing that can be done to make things better. Consequently, they are resigned to this outcome because their passive-aggressiveness eliminates any opportunity to discover alternatives.

Goleman states that "people who experience chronic anxiety, long periods of sadness and pessimism, unremitting tension or incessant hostility, relentless cynicism or suspiciousness, were found to have double the risk of disease."[11] On the other side of the coin, a degree of healing power evolves because optimists are better at bearing up under difficult circumstances.

Most adults who love a child want them to grow up without a victim mentality and its pessimistic and manipulative dysfunctions. Parents and educators have to ensure that they are appropriate models for children in facing issues.

While happiness is a goal, life has another dimension—joy. Few discussions center on joy. In speaking with older citizens, love is discussed as the key to happiness and within that is the joy in spending time with loved ones.

Seeing children take their first step or speak their first word is joyful. "Joy is a connection to the universe"[12] —an emotion. It is not egocentric but is more altruistically and affectionately connected to others.

Joy is truly heartfelt and is a feeling parents hope their children experience. "Joy is inward, it is generated inside. It is not found outside and brought in. It is for those who accept the world as it is, part good, part bad, and who identify with the good by adding a little island of serenity to it."[13]

Victim mentality is a life sentence in which happiness is not pursued and one that causes serious breaks in social and work relationships. Learning and growth is curtailed, and skills and aptitudes are constricted. Maturation is sidelined because responsibility and accountability are rejected. Finally, the egocentric view of life—"poor me"—results in isolation and limitations in finding not only happiness but also joy.

The continued well-being of children and adults rests on both meaning and happiness. Individuals living in accord with their values and calling find satisfaction and happiness. Self-reliance brings personal control and the power to make choices that can change circumstances and alter an individual's life.

Each person chooses how they live, and hopefully, they do it with maturity and wisdom. Maturity and wisdom are complementary. Mature people use sound judgment and solid reasoning based on values and convictions. Wise choices require active involvement and honor commitments and principles. Planning beyond the immediate moment or the pressure of peers is important for making wise decisions.

Today, with social and political stereotyping, this is not always easy, particularly for those in their teens and as young adults trying to make their way. Wise adults behave authentically in harmony with their values and do not stand behind pretense. Sensitivity to their principles and the needs of others is important, and humility is a virtue.

Maturity requires acceptance of responsibility and learning to deal with failure. Gardner defines the attributes of mature individuals as:[14]

- understanding mutual dependence and mutual commitments
- creating their own environment
- balancing individuality and commitments beyond themselves and to the community

- having to "be" as well as "do"
- letting go and taking their hands off the world at times
- understanding the path of life may be as important as the destination

Gardner states:

> Meaning is not something you stumble across, like the answer to a riddle or the prize in a treasure hunt. Meaning is something you build into your life. You build it out of your past, out of your affections and loyalties, out of the experience of humankind as it is passed on to you, out of your own talent and understanding, out of the things you believe in, out of the things in the people you love, out of the values for which you are willing to sacrifice something.
>
> The ingredients are there. You are the only one who can put them together into that unique pattern that will be your life. Let it be a life that has dignity and meaning for you. If it does, then the particular balance of success or failure—as the world measures success or failure—is of less account.[15]

When all is said and done, everyone wants to be happy and find purpose in life—both concern well-being. If individuals live in ways that are meaningful and emblematic of who they really are, then happiness and satisfaction follow. Discovering that they fit in the world and finding significance in life are what people and children dream about as they think about the future.

At the end of life, individuals want to know what difference their lives meant—"Why was I here?" Happiness alone does not result in significance. It takes character.

POINTS TO REMEMBER

- Victim mentality limits growth and is cancerous to relationships, individual development, and ultimately society.
- Victim mentality stymies living with meaning and pursuing happiness.
- Happiness and meaning are not synonymous. Happiness relates to having needs met, while meaning involves self-understanding and discovering one's own path.
- Meaning has two components: cognitive processing (making sense of circumstances) and purpose (pursuing goals related to self-identity).
- Everyone has the ability and freedom to choose how they respond—positively or negatively—to conditions and circumstances.
- Knowing the "why" of life furnishes the reason and responsibility to live it.
- Meaning can be found through suffering and success. Failure has it benefits and can produce wisdom if individuals perceive it as part of the pathway of life.
- Meaning is a major factor in well-being. Living to please others is hollow.

- Finding purpose and meaning can lead to joy.
- Maturity involves living with responsibility, balancing commitments, and understanding that the path of life may be as important as the destination.

NOTES

1. Fred Kofman, *Conscious Business: How to Build Value through Values* (Boulder, CO: Sounds True, 2006), Kindle edition, 17.
2. Scott Barry Kaufman, "The Differences between Happiness and Meaning in Life," *Scientific American Blog Network*, January 30, 2016, https://blogs.scientificamerican.com/beautiful-minds/the-differences-between-happiness-and-meaning-in-life.
3. Thomas Lickona, *Character Matters* (New York: Touchstone, 2004), Kindle edition, 3–4.
4. Mihaly Csikszentmihalyi, *Flow* (New York: HarperCollins, 2008), Kindle edition, 112–17.
5. Viktor Frankl, *Man's Search for Meaning* (New York: Washington Square Press, 1984), 133.
6. Lickona, *Character Matters*, 8.
7. J. K. Rowling, "The Fringe Benefits of Failure, and the Importance of Imagination," speech, Cambridge, MA, June 5, 2008, *Harvard Gazette*, http://news.harvard.edu/gazette/story/2008/06/text-of-j-k-rowling-speech/.
8. Viktor Frankl, *The Will to Meaning* (New York: Penguin, 1988), 167.
9. Joseph Campbell, *Joseph Campbell: Reflections on the Art of Living*, ed. Diane K. Osbon (New York: Harper Perennial, 1991), 22.
10. Csikszentmihalyi, *Flow*, 3.
11. Daniel Goleman, *Emotional Intelligence* (New York: Random House, 2012), Kindle edition, 168.
12. George Vaillant, *Spiritual Evolution* (New York: Broadway Books, 2008), 124.
13. Robert K. Greenleaf, *Servant Leadership* (New York: Paulist Press, 1997), 57.
14. John Gardner, *Living, Leading, and the American Dream* (San Francisco: Jossey-Bass, 2003), 55–56.
15. Ibid., 53.

Chapter Five

Character Matters

"People grow through experience if they meet life honestly and courageously. This is how character is built." —Eleanor Roosevelt

"Parents can only give good advice or put them on the right paths, but the final forming of a person's character lies in their own hands." —Anne Frank

America's myths, folklore, and legends reinforce its principles. To paraphrase John Winthrop's words, "the shining city on a hill" has been a metaphor for America and its democratic values, as well as the opportunity it represents. These values raise and define expectations and opportunities for all individuals. Academics and knowledge can be dangerous without character, as totalitarian regimes have proved. History is replete with examples.

Revolutionary War figures such as Patrick Henry and his reported comment "Give me liberty or give me death" exemplified the revolution and its purpose. Even the tall tales of Davy Crockett, John Henry, Molly Pitcher, and fictional characters like Paul Bunyan and the Lone Ranger have similar themes—liberty and justice and standing up and overcoming challenges. All are American symbols of how citizens should react to situations and cope with life's complexities.

Stories and myths, while sometimes based on fictional characters or events, direct American's inclinations and aspirations. Cultural characters tell a larger story based on principles, but they also carry the expectation of personal responsibility.

Americans are characterized as succeeding against the odds through straight talk and a "can-do" attitude as told in historic events and through individuals who stood forthright for honorable causes. Martin Luther King stated, "We shall overcome," which reverberated throughout the country.

Inherent in this movement was optimism and the ability to face difficult social issues, get to work, and stand firm for values.

Americans are generally optimistic about the future, believing that collective action can improve conditions and overcome obstacles. President Franklin Roosevelt in his first inaugural address in 1933, given in the depths of the Depression, stated, "The only thing we have to fear is fear itself."

Citizens were called to confront and act to solve the challenges and perilous circumstances of economic collapse and not become paralyzed in their thinking or behavior. Confidence, not fear, is the nation's mantra: optimism that things can change through individual and collective action.

Independence and rugged individualism and a stand-up-and-be-counted attitude are inherent in being a self-governing society founded on the ideal of free expression. To maintain the image of the shining city on the hill, Americans are expected to live these qualities and apply their abilities.

The belief in progress through hard work and self-confidence liberates people to collectively pursue happiness. In society, citizens are free to respond to situations individually and collectively to create innovations and to model our national values. Each individual matters, not external powers or the government: citizens are free to autonomously direct their lives and make choices.

HEROES

Today's media touts celebrities, stars, and "heroes"—all aimed at young people. Madison Avenue advertising and image buffing fabricates these so-called stars and heroes, often confusing celebrity and character.

Children select heroes to emulate. Obviously, some will be athletes, musicians, actors, and the like. Hopefully, they choose more than pop culture types. Fame does not always equate with integrity, character, or intelligence.

The issue is the nature of the character of their heroes. Do they exemplify initiative and personal responsibility? In some cases, today's so-called heroes are talented and skilled but lack the maturity to conduct themselves with humility or moral integrity. Others cut legal corners, and some set negative examples of behavior, relationships, or lifestyle through destructive and egocentric conduct.

Our culture emphasizes self-promotion—"Look at me!" Even children with a victim mentality garner the spotlight through self-pitying manipulation. Social media is an outlet for self-promotion—selfies, tweets, texts, and websites. Creating a "brand" and personality is often marketed to obtain "likes" and "followers"—a "brand" is not character.

Self-reflection gets buried as individuals scurry for attention and to accumulate friends. Humility is frequently lost and results in self-satisfied mediocrity. Time is squandered technologically by the constant hawking of personal and trivial activities and responding to others' minutiae-laden day-to-day exploits, feelings, or opinions.

Self-discipline and adherence to principle are at the core of character. People's character affects children whether they experience them face-to-face or observe their behavior or learn about it in history and literature. As children get older, their own personal and family histories reveal people of character who influenced them and made an impact because of their principles and conduct or lack thereof.

Heroism and honor frequently are demonstrated in small, quiet acts of standing on principle in the face of adversity or challenge. Bravery is not always as Hollywood interprets and depicts it. Most frequently, teachers, colleagues, or community or family members demonstrate it in solitary and decisive resolve through individualism and doing the "right" thing.

Character is not about image or achievement but involves ethical and moral behavior, integrity, and courage that exemplify the inner nature of a person. Individuals are tested through dilemmas, challenges, and enigmas. Unexpected questions and realities from acts of fate or personal attitudes and actions occur, requiring difficult choices to be made that may be life changing.

Single parents persevere despite difficult economic conditions so they can raise their children as well as possible. They become beacons of strength for their children. Teachers take the time to become "polestars" and provide guidance, support, and honesty in giving firm but loving feedback to help students see themselves from another confident perspective.

Grandparents, uncles, aunts, mothers, or fathers stand up when needed on matters of decency and honor at home, in the neighborhood, or at work. Neighbors assist others in difficult times even when not convenient and sometimes at personal expense. They all do so under the radar from the general population but are pivotal in helping other people grow and overcome.

National figures have demonstrated courage and character. Conversely, history illustrates intelligent individuals standing by and doing nothing in the face of treachery or personal risk. In politics, political figures and notables from both political parties parse words, obfuscate former decisions and performance, and expound outright lies, half-truths, and deception. Being smart and knowledgeable is hollow without the character to stand on noble principles. Appearances and images are not always reflective of reality.

People and groups who were underdogs rose to the challenge, succeeded, and overcame the odds. The historic 1980 Olympic hockey team, ranked to finish sixth, upset the powerful Russians and went on to win a gold medal. Why? Character, discipline, and hard work were nonnegotiable expectations of the coach, Herb Brooks, who provided clear and firm guidance.

He was quoted as telling his players, "You think you can win on talent alone. You don't have enough talent to win on talent alone" and, of course, the notable, "The name on the front of the sweater [uniform] is more important than the one on the back." Even with highly accomplished athletes, it takes more than skill and talent—hard work, commitment, and teamwork were the keys. Character and pushing beyond self-defined limits can alter attitudes and events.

In political history, there are others such as Rosa Parks, who, through principle and resolve, highlighted injustice by simply and symbolically taking a seat on a bus against convention and social expectation. She is quoted as saying, "You must never be fearful about what you are doing when it is right." She believed in living life as a model for others, as did Susan B. Anthony, who stood firmly for suffrage rights and was an active abolitionist before the Civil War.

American history and mythology are filled with stories of character and heroism in the face of moral, physical, or emotional challenges. American character has historically been grounded in resilience, grit, independence, and courage.

Literature, film, and theater convey stories of individuals confronting conflict and dilemmas. Sometimes they overcome and sometimes not. At times victory is given a different face than expected, and even in failure individuals succeed because of the challenge they faced and weathered, despite falling short. Raising principled awareness, even against the odds to bring about change, is an act of character.

Screenwriters and playwrights create fictional characters that confront almost impossible odds and survive. Rocky Balboa, an everyman, long-shot, "meat and potatoes" fighter in the *Rocky* film series, is one iconic example who went from an unknown to a contender for the heavyweight championship.

These films attract audiences because they appeal to people's imagination, lives, historical values, and ideals. They engage them emotionally. In one of the films, Rocky gives a powerful speech to his son that exemplifies American lore, ideals, and ethos. He states:

> Let me tell you something you already know. The world ain't all sunshine and rainbows. It is a very mean and nasty place and it will beat you to your knees and keep you there permanently if you let it. You, me, or nobody is gonna hit as hard as life. But it ain't how hard you hit; it's about how hard you can get hit, and keep moving forward. How much you can take, and keep moving forward. That's how winning is done. Now, if you know what you're worth, then go out and get what you're worth. But you gotta be willing to take the hit, and not pointing fingers. Saying you ain't where you are because of him, or her, or anybody. Cowards do that and that ain't you. You're better than that![1]

In essence, Rocky asserts that adopting a victim mentality is a path to collapse and defeat. Facing life and overcoming adversity seems like a piece of fiction for those who assume that position. They are not willing to take the hit, and they continue to assert that they have no responsibility for the aftermath.

Some people have false assumptions about life's challenges. Everyone wants to protect those they love from difficulty and pain; however, it is fallacious for children to believe that they will be protected from some of the inevitabilities and hardships of life. As poet David Whyte wrote, "Magical Thinking [is] the belief that somehow we will be exempt from grief and losses that have afflicted others and that somehow, because of our special knowledge, we will be protected."[2]

A more powerful message to children is that in the face of eventual adversity and failure, they are not powerless. They can act. They can stand up. They have a voice. Confronting anxiety, pain, trouble, and failure actually can strengthen their sense of competence and character.

People with character do not fade in the face of problems and trouble but step up even against the odds. "A sense of worth, mastery, or self-esteem cannot be bestowed. It can only be earned. If it is given away, it ceases to be worth having, and it ceases to contribute to individual dignity. If we remove obstacles, difficulties, anxiety, and competition from the lives of our young people, we may no longer see generations of young people who have a sense of dignity, power, and worth."[3]

Ricky was a ten-year-old fifth grader whose father died when he was four years old. He was a bit shy and hesitant to participate in outside activities. Confidence was not his long suit. His mother was a short-order cook in a diner and was responsible for raising him and his sister.

Ricky saw a poster in school about Little League tryouts. He used to play catch with his cousin—pitching and catching—and was a Chicago Cubs fan, although he never saw a professional game. So he took his ball and mitt and went to the tryout.

He really didn't know what position he wanted to play, and after a few errors, dropped balls, and missed plays, he was assigned to right field. After a while, the boys were called in and stood around second base waiting for the coaches' decisions.

The three coaches huddled together within earshot of Ricky. He heard one say: "What about Ricky? Not too skilled. Doesn't understand the game. Not ready, we should cut him."

"Well, I don't know. I heard the kid's father died a couple years ago. He can't play worth beans, no skills, pretty bad really . . . but I'll take him."

Ricky stood there, heard the comments, picked up his glove, and walked home. The coaches' words lingered in his head. Although they were well intentioned, hearing them had a negative effect. He didn't want sympathy. He could experience failure but did not want to win because of sympathy. He wanted a chance, not pity or a handout. He wanted to earn it: a value he was taught by his mother.

DREAM OR REALITY?

Americans have always been dreamers. Freedom. Justice. Opportunity. All of these can seem like dreams to some, particularly in autocratic environments. But dreams give the impression of effortlessness and ease. This certainly is not the case, particularly with the American Dream, which requires great effort, stamina, and hard work. It is not without suffering and hardship. Persevering in the face of hardship is the standard, as well as courage to look at faults and flaws and try to change them. There are many smart and intelligent people who cannot stand the press of events, conflict of values, or harsh debate.

We can dream of great outcomes and happy endings, but without the character to get involved and learn from experience, nothing will happen or change. Accepting the role as innocent "bystander" is part of the problem. Even if actions fail, virtue can live and survive. Dietrich Bonhoeffer, the German theologian and an active Nazi dissident who was put to death just before the end of the war, states, "Things do exist that are worth standing up for without compromise. To me it seems that peace and social justice are such things."[4]

Living up to responsibilities, and assuming accountability, requires people to take action and do the things required of citizens, family members, employees, or neighbors. Vaclav Havel states, "Democracy is a system based on trust in the human sense of responsibility, which it ought to awaken and cultivate. . . . Today, when our very planetary civilization is endangered by irresponsibility, I see no other way to save it than through a general awakening and cultivation of a sense of responsibility people have for the affairs of this world."[5]

Addressing responsibilities, however, is not a guarantee of success. "There is no guarantee that what you do will yield what you want. The guarantee is that as long as you are alive and conscious, you can respond to your circumstances in pursuit of your happiness. This power to respond is a defining feature of humanity. Our response-ability is a direct expression of our rationality, our will, and our freedom. Being human is being responsible."[6]

Fulfilling responsibilities requires individuals to consider that they may be part of the problem but with the understanding that they are also part of the solution. Becoming accountable is an integral part of character; otherwise, speaking out can be nothing more than insincere and empty rhetoric.

Character matters for each individual but also for the community and society as a whole. Decency, order, and justice are all dependent on people acting with character and integrity and sense of duty. It relates specifically to a moral standard of conduct and the common good. Standing by as a self-imposed victim is destructive to that idea. Victim mentality is the antithesis of acting with character.

CHARACTER

Attitudes today are different from the mid-1960s. "In 1966, 80% of freshman said that they were strongly motivated to develop a meaningful philosophy of life. Today, less than half say that. In 1966, 42% said that becoming rich was an important life goal. By 1990, 74% agreed with that statement."[7]

Over time, self-promotion and an "I" orientation and focus have superseded words like "community" and "common good." "Me" is spotlighted today and there is a sense of "specialness." Brooks contends that children are "praised" to an unprecedented degree and "incessantly told how special they are."[8] In addition, Gough indicates that an abundance of self-esteem can result in unethical and antisocial behavior.[9]

Humility and honesty, along with courage, are important in addressing challenges and defeat. Quiet reflection is a significant tool to understand how and why events happened as they did. Sometimes pure reason is not sufficient. Self-understanding is powerful in finding a new way to address situations and the fortitude to move ahead.

In a real sense, character, not personality or self-esteem, defines a person's destiny. In their book *Character Strengths and Virtues*, Peterson and Seligman identify the six core virtues that underwrite character: courage, justice, humanity, temperance, transcendence, and wisdom.[10] They indicate that a life well-lived is based on the foundation of these strengths that provide stability of purpose and define the virtues for a meaningful life.

Character strengths help individuals cope with adversity but also help fulfill a person's life. Each strength is important and has a purpose in its own right. Collectively, these strengths augment positive attitudes in society, as well as enhance the life of each person individually.

People of character are examples for others. They are not "goody two shoes" or smug individuals. Their values guide them—not for superiority over others or for the sake of notoriety or recognition, but because the strengths manifest their individual thoughts, feelings, and actions.

Character strengths are in stark contrast to those who adopt a victim mentality and a passive and despondent role. These strengths provide the basis for building and responding to life and are the foundation for persistence, hard work, and self-control.

Character strengths are desired in colleagues, leaders, and relationships. Parents desire these traits in their children. Employers and neighbors like these qualities in the people with whom they work. "Good character is not the absence of deficits and problems, but rather a well-developed family of positive traits."[11] They have a moral dimension to them, which encourages and results in virtuous behavior.

The character strengths identified by Peterson and Seligman help young men and women uncover a satisfying pathway to find solutions and meaning. These strengths provide support and a sense of direction, as well as help people get through adversity and challenges with fewer psychological or physical problems.[12]

MINDSETS AND CHARACTER

An individual's mindset determines how they view life. "Be careful of your thoughts, for your thoughts become your words. Be careful of your words, for your words become your deeds. Be careful of your deeds, for your deeds become your habits. Be careful of your habits, for your habits become your character."[13] The victim mentality freezes the mind into a mold of irresponsible disempowerment and resentment.

Mindsets affect the way people live. A growth mindset "is based on the belief that your basic qualities are things you can cultivate through your efforts. . . . Everyone can change and grow through application and experience."[14] The character strengths presume an active and responsible attitude.

People with a growth mindset seek challenges and know that progress takes time to blossom. They are not deterred by setbacks or falling short. Success comes from engagement, giving the best effort, and learning and improving. A negative or fixed mindset stunts learning and experience because of the fear of failure.

One consistent facet of life is change. We see it economically, technologically, culturally, and personally. Everyone wrestles with these changes to find their way, maintain their integrity, and grow and learn. Monitoring what is happening and being sensitive to how change affects them is important. In changing circumstances, victims expect to be losers and fall into apathy or perceive others as their problem.

Individuals with character and a growth mindset are self-aware and know what is happening to them externally and internally. They practice self-acceptance and manage their emotions without judgment. They self-regulate and have the capacity to subordinate self-gratification. Self-control and self-inquiry requires getting at the root causes of emotions and motivation.

The Greek philosopher Heraclitus stated, "Character is destiny." The values, principles, and ethics individuals live by create the framework around which they make choices. Character begins with self-understanding: what they stand for, how they act, and how they face life. Knowing "thyself" is the basis for how individuals use their autonomy.

Children must recognize that their character defines them, not their appearance, their socioeconomic status, their family structure, their racial or ethnic background, or other factors. Thoughts, words, and deeds express who they are as individuals, and actions and demeanor communicate clearly the content of a person's character far more than where they are from or their lineage.

People of good character exemplify the virtues of honesty, courage, compassion, and justice. Students should study these virtues and discuss them. In reality, they establish the bedrock for goodness, a trait parents almost universally want their children to have.

Character is present, exposed, and lived every day in school. It is often a part of the hidden curriculum, which is not explicitly spelled out but is encountered socially and personally because it is embodied in relationships and social interactions. This hidden curriculum is about "being"—being an individual, being a part of a class, and being in interaction with teachers and others.

The hidden curriculum is experienced in all facets of a child's life—at home, socially, or in the neighborhood. They are observing and acting. They are exposed to power and are faced with the expectations of others—some good and some bad. They must act and learn in this context: their actions are either emblematic of resilience or of a casualty.

The virtues behind character are passed down to children from teachers, parents, and other adults. Certainly, they are passed from generation to generation. Character is associated with honor, duty, and integrity and is based on moral discipline—not ego, self-interest, or desires.

The autonomy children and adults desire has two components: responsibility and accountability for their actions. Autonomy requires taking responsibility, as well as facing accountability for decisions and action.

CHARACTER AND TRAGEDIES

At times, events are so difficult and beyond understanding that getting through them seems impossible, incomprehensible, deadening to thought and soul. These are days when the world changes. For children, these life-changing events can alter their mindscapes and futures. Critical events impact perspective and become some of the most painful and stressful turning points.

Tragedies—particularly deaths—are life altering for children and their relationships and perspective. They don't have the experience and maturity to even comprehend what death is or how to deal with it. "More than anything else, the death of a parent marks the end of childhood."[15] The child can grow up feeling different and alone.

A tragedy of this magnitude shatters the assumptions about how the world works and is not always understandable to children or youth. Beliefs about safety, parental power, and reality are shattered. From their perspective, death is supposed to happen in the later stages of life, not when they are kids.

Getting through an unthinkable tragedy, which will be a vivid part of them for the rest of their lives, is not easy. One would presume that a victim mentality would be the norm.

Yet in many cases, these children build a barrier of self-reliance—an attitude of "I can do it myself." Independence and building on the strengths of courage, humanity, transcendence, and wisdom help them move ahead with life, not by eliminating their memories, but by using them to grow and learn.

An example of character strengths in a young person is in Claire Bower's speech for Every Mother Counts, a nonprofit organization that model Christy Turlington founded dedicated to safe childbirth and maternal health. She invited Claire to speak at a benefit in New York City. This is what Claire, a sixteen-year-old junior in high school, said:

> Mothers nurture and care for their children, help them develop their first opinions, teach them good values, and educate them in the ways of life. But what about children without living mothers?
>
> Naturally, the lucky ones have relatives, or friends, that step in and take on the roles of the mother, but the child still has to live without the closeness of a maternal figure. There will always be a void that remains within the child as they lack the bond with their mother. Learning to live, grow, and help others with this void is what becomes important as these children grow up.
>
> A month before my fourth birthday, my own mother passed away due to a childbirth complication that presented itself while she was in labor with my younger brother, Luke. As you can imagine, this rocked my world. I vividly remember the last conversation I had with her, how I was told of her passing, and the memories of frequent park adventures and Disney trips. The closeness with her evaporated without warning.
>
> Growing up was hard. There is no way possible to sugarcoat that; I would be lying if I said it was easy. Birthdays, becoming a teenager, my first school dance, Christmas (my mother's favorite holiday), learning to become a confident young woman, dating, these are some of the simple things that showed to be particularly bittersweet growing up. I was happy with their presence, but saddened by the lack of my mother's. It's always the simple things we take for granted that stick with us the most . . . or at least that's what I've found to be true for myself.

The current struggle is advice. Many young girls turn to their mothers for comfort, wise words, or laughter in the midst of anxiety. While I have many loving people around me that I appreciate, there are times that the little girl inside of me yearns to sit and get guidance from her own mother. To hear her opinion, to have her hug me and tell me, "It's going to be okay," to guide me in looking for colleges as a junior and senior in high school, and into the quickly approaching transition from a teenager to a college-aged adult.

For many children, I feel it's the steady rhythm of daily life with their mother that they miss. Once she is gone the beat simply is not the same and their life is all of a sudden a completely different tune.

Among small children the saying "Get over it!" is often thrown around, and when you think about it, that saying is entirely ridiculous. People cannot control how they feel. Individuals can control how they react and use their emotions, but they cannot control the emotions that their brain creates and presents.

So honestly, telling somebody to get over an unfortunate event is absurd. Typically, people don't like to feel sad, angry, or depressed, so I'm sure they would "get over it" in an instant if they had it their way; this is important to keep in mind at all times when dealing with anybody that has lost anyone of importance in their life.

On another note, it is crucial that grieving individuals know it is okay to be mourning. When I was growing up, sometimes I would try to suppress my own emotions simply so that I would feel strong and like I had accomplished something, when truly, ignoring the reality of my emotions and failing to face them head on accomplished absolutely nothing but prolonged heartache. Learning to face the emotions, the heartache, and the loss was a day-to-day learning process but one that has made me who I am today.

As a young child, I was blessed to have a large group of people in my life that were constantly there to love, encourage, and rally around me to raise me up. This helped to give me confidence and provide the maternal affection I otherwise couldn't receive. These people did not ignore my mother's existence or her death; they didn't shove the facts under the rug. The people who knew my mother recognized her life and were open with sharing her opinions, experiences, and passions with me as I grew up. So though I could not grow up with my mother physically present, her ideas and life story still impacted and influenced me every day. I will forever be grateful for that.

Furthermore, none of these people forced me to talk about my feelings, they did not suffocate me with treatment, they did not interrogate me about my emotions, they provided a constant love and were incredibly respectful of the things I was comfortable and uncomfortable with. This was critical in my growth as I learned to trust those around me, how to cope with my own emotions in a healthy manner, and it also allowed me to truly take the time I needed to work through the grieving process. Every person has different needs in traumatic situations; these needs must also be respected and taken into consideration. It is the only way for any help to be effective and for the individual to grow, learn, and work past their negative state.

The loss of my mother taught me many things about life, one of which being the fact that in one second everything can change, and entire situations, families, and environments can be altered. As I've gotten older, this has become a constant theme in my daily life. I strive to always look at the bigger picture and live looking forward, using every second I have.

Moreover, it taught me that through hardships we must find courage, confront our own emotions, grow wise through experience, and learn to cope with the situation so that we do not live the rest of our lives dwelling within a shadow of loss. These lessons have made me strong and have given me a much different perspective of the concept of life, along with its purpose.

As a sixteen-year-old, I am making it my mission to do as much as I can to build others up, advocate for maternal safety, promote equality globally, and to work to make the entire international community a safer place, both physically and emotionally for all. Every conversation that spreads awareness, every little bit of love you give to others, everything you pour into current issues makes a difference, regardless of what the issue is. As cliché as it sounds, finding something to fight for, finding a purpose, being able to help someone that otherwise cannot help themselves—that is kindness, that is love, that is compassion, that is what humanity should be.

Growing up without my biological mother was not easy, but it did teach me something. I cannot change what has happened to me, but I can take the negative things that have happened in the past sixteen years, and I can consciously choose to use them to make a positive impact and find a purpose. If using my story and what I have learned from my experience to spread awareness can help one person, it has helped somebody and I have served a purpose. That is what is now important to me.

I encourage all young women like myself, and all young men, to use their experiences to grow, use their hardships to learn, and to use their lives for good. At the end of your life, will you be proud of what you did and who you impacted? That is what we all must ask ourselves. So let's all step out, find our purpose, and fulfill it.

When Claire's story is analyzed, character strengths and self-reflection are evident. In her case, it would be easy to fall into a victim mentality: despairing and giving up on creating a life for herself. She survived the worst possible thing that could happen to a child. She had to develop a "self"—without her mother—to guide her. Many children who survive trauma feel strengthened by their triumph over adversity. They become aware of the strength to manage life and often, as Claire indicates, want to commit their lives to a social good.

"Your life is your message."[16] Character translates the message to others. The principles on which people stand send a definitive message about their value and whether they live with integrity. Personal responsibility, truth, love, respect, and courage are essential parts of that message. Living with ideals nourishes not only minds but also souls. Living truthfully in dealing with others and treating others with love and dignity results in a life well lived.

POINTS TO REMEMBER

- Character is not about fame and notoriety. It involves ethical and moral conduct, integrity to principles and values, and courage to act on them even in the face of opposition.
- In the face of adversity and failure, children are not powerless. Obstacles, anxiety, and competition can be addressed through behaving with character, dignity, and self-worth.
- Autonomy requires individuals to make ethical decisions in the face of choices presented by peers, circumstances, or personal desires. Wisdom is an essential quality in exercising autonomy and formulating decisions.
- Standing on the sidelines as a self-designated victim is destructive to a sense of character. Character requires living up to responsibilities and assuming accountability.
- Character defines destiny.
- The character strengths of courage, justice, humanity, temperance, transcendence, and wisdom are components of a resilient life well-lived.
- An individual's mindset determines how they view life in the way they live. People with a growth mindset are not deterred by setbacks. Those with a fixed mindset of fear and failure see things rigidly.
- A tragedy, like the death of a parent or others, is life changing for children and shatters the assumptions they held for how the world works.
- Helping children through difficult times includes: providing constant love, respecting the things they are comfortable and uncomfortable with, developing trust with children so they can cope with their emotions in a healthy manner.
- Children cannot always change what happens to them, but they can choose to use circumstances to find a mission, purpose, and meaning.

NOTES

1. Sylvester Stallone, *Rocky Balboa* (Beverly Hills, CA: Metro-Goldwyn-Mayer, 2006).
2. David Whyte, *The Heart Aroused* (New York: Currency Doubleday, 1994), 34.
3. Martin E. P. Seligman, *Helplessness* (San Francisco: W. H. Freeman and Company, 1975), 159.
4. Eric Metaxas, *Bonhoeffer: Pastor, Martyr, Prophet, Spy* (Nashville: Thomas Nelson, 2010), 260.
5. Vaclav Havel, *The Art of the Impossible* (New York: Knopf, 1997), 145.
6. Fred Kofman, *Conscious Business: How to Build Value through Values* (Boulder, CO: Sounds True, 2006), 31.
7. James D. Hunter, *The Death of Character* (New York: Basic Books, 2000), 7.
8. David Brooks, *The Road to Character* (New York: Random House, 2015), Kindle edition, 257.
9. Russell W. Gough, *Character Is Destiny* (Rocklin, CA: Prima Publishing, 1997), 9–10.
10. Christopher Peterson and Martin E. P. Seligman, *Character Strengths and Virtues* (New York: Oxford University Press, 2004), 12–37.

11. Nansook Park and Christopher Peterson, "Character Strengths: Research and Practice," *Journal of College and Character* 10, no. 4 (April 2009): 1.

12. Ibid., 8.

13. Thomas Likona, *Character Matters* (New York: Touchstone, 2004), 3.

14. Carol Dweck, *Mindset: New Psychology of Success* (New York: Random House, 2006), 7.

15. Maxine Harris, *The Loss That Is Forever* (New York: Penguin, 1996), 10.

16. Keshavan Nair, *A Higher Standard of Leadership* (San Francisco: Berrett-Koehler, 1994), 140.

Chapter Six

Being and Self-Efficacy

> "We pay a heavy price for our fear of failure. It is a powerful obstacle to growth. It assures the progressive narrowing of the personality and prevents exploration and experimentation. There is no learning without some difficulty and fumbling. If you want to keep on learning, you must keep on risking failure—all your life. It's as simple as that." —John Gardner

Success! All facets of our culture tout success. Get in the right college and prosperity will follow. "Let us invest your money and your future is secured," investment bankers proclaim. Got a weight problem? Just adopt our new diet plan and never give up the food you enjoy and you'll shed pounds. Political commercials, complete with beautiful sunrise pictures, peddle a successful future for you and your family if you just elect "fill in the blank."

Most definitions of success concern prosperity, winning, and triumph. Our culture hypes stardom, superstardom, megastars, and, of course, a litany of celebrities, VIPs, and dignitaries. Failure is not an option. Individuals fear a reputation as a failure, particularly having it publicized.

Success is usually tied to tangible outcomes. Efforts that do not produce desired results are fiascos according to pop culture and contemporary social norms. In this vein, great effort without the triumph ends up as a "lead balloon"—a defeat usually perceived as a useless flop.

Ironically, sometimes failure produces results. For example, the breakfast cereal Wheaties was a result of a mishap of spilling gruel on a hot stove. Other mistakes resulted in plastics, and in medicine. A messy lab bench and dirty Petri dish led to the development of penicillin. Taking a wrong resistor out of a box of equipment resulted in the pacemaker. Edison tried more than nine thousand kinds of filaments before he found the one that worked.

In science, the World Health Organization has called for the publication of negative findings in clinical research trials. Its position is that reporting them can help colleagues from wasting time and resources by repeating negative trials and results. Knowing what isn't effective or significant is very important and might eventually lead to a favorable outcome.

Winning, or the specter of it, is what parents and students want. In fact, we give trophies, pens, and certificates for everything, including just showing up. Some say only true "winners" should get trophies. Others worry about the self-concept of those who played the game but did not prevail or excel. They think they should be recognized for trying and effort. Winning seems to be everything to some parents: just look at their bumper stickers flaunting honor roll attainment.

The scoreboard was running down to the last thirty seconds—Warhawks 2, Huskies 4.

The coach met the team in the locker room after the game and said, "Well, boys, we played a good game. Great effort and teamwork today. I know this is a tough loss. Just remember: the sun will come out tomorrow morning. This is just a game. What counts is that you give everything you got during the game. That's what you did today! Good character, boys!"

He walked out of the locker room where the parents were waiting. He went up to Mrs. Wilton and said, "Eddie played a good game today. He was our best player, particularly in our zone."

"But we lost!" she said. "He didn't score a goal. How can you say he was the best player today? Curtis scored both goals."

"Mrs. Wilton—he was our strongest player. He played good offense and defense . . . both sides of the rink. He was a positive leader and led the team—never gave up the whole game. You don't have to score to be the best player."

She stared at him and said, "I have higher standards than that. I expect excellence from my son."

"Then," the coach said, "you better understand what playing the game is about. Sometimes scoring goals is not the most difficult part of the game. It's about character, resiliency, leadership."

The question is: Why do we need trophies and why is the outcome of a kids' hockey game perceived to be a matter of life and death? Is it just to create winners and losers? What about work ethic—persevering against the odds, doing your best, and commitment? What about integrity and fortitude? Winning or succeeding in spurious ways is hollow and not a victory at all if it is based on deception, ego, or dishonesty. Integrity and values matter in how children participate.

Effort and determination count in and out of competitive activities. Playing the game and doing the work right is important in all facets of life. Resilience—the ability to confront and bounce back from adversity—is essential because there are no pristine, unsullied lives. Whether in personal or business circumstances, flexible responses may be necessary.

Sometimes situations require careful and rigorous uphill plodding. Succeeding in some cases may take quite a long time—months or even years. Noble causes or personal reformations are not achieved instantaneously. Character is indispensable in any line of work and is as important as mastering and applying knowledge.

When facing daily life, character and the ability to recover are absolutely vital in extreme, painful, and unthinkable situations. Persevering and being adaptable and maintaining values and principles are not always easy. Heartbreak can twist logic and push people to breaking points. Surviving the circumstances, moving ahead, and maintaining wholeness takes courage and strength. These situations affect both adults' and children's being and behavior.

DOING AND BEING

The focus of life usually is on "doings": producing or making something and completing tasks or projects that require competence, fervor, and talent. In organizations, "doing" is valued and usually enforced through hierarchical expectations and regulations. "Doing" has a task orientation and concerns physical and mental activity.

The other side of life is "being": embracing the present and self-acceptance for who one is, not for what one does. Values are relationship oriented: inclusion, compassion, acceptance, and care. "We are human beings, not human doings. Our 'being' is our integral wholeness—mind, body, spirit, and soul. As beings, we are unique—we have a presence all our own, and no two of us are alike. We have distinct energy that can be seen and felt as part of our presence by letting what's inside of us come out, rather than externally posturing and positioning ourselves to win approval."[1]

Individuals obviously "do" things—they make choices, create things, and accomplish something tangible. "Being," on the other hand, concerns accepting themselves as individuals and taking responsibility for their lives. In that regard, they decide why they make decisions, how they make them, and to what end. "Being" drives who people really are—titles, money, or awards, in reality, do not. "Being" encompasses values, beliefs, and an ethical disposition that is demonstrated in behavior.

Both "being" and "doing" are important, but "being" drives the other in terms of dedication to principles and standards. The kind of person individuals desire to be is basic to their "being." Do they remain conscious of their values and responsibilities and refuse to compromise them for material success or for the sake of seeking pity or the recognition of others? Do they speak truth and listen to others with respect and honesty to develop important creative solutions?

Having a victim mentality disparages both "being" and "doing" and prevents the possibility of responding to events with any sense of character. Their "being" is inauthentic and "doing" is absent. For self-perpetuating victims, long-term planning is nonexistent.[2] Responsibility is deflected. Blaming is prevalent, along with the attitude that they are "owed" something. Those with victim mentality pretend not to have any connection to the situation they are in. Wallowing in problems and stagnating are endemic, as are distorting circumstances and failing to accept any culpability.

This attitude diminishes their sense of character. Their attitudes and behavior are frozen the way they are, which deflates their sense of being. Motivation is foiled, resulting in feeling sorry for themselves. Anger is at the base of much of this behavior. People are separated into good ones and bad ones, and no attempt is made to consider the point of view of others.

The opposite of victim mentality is having an accountability mentality: a sense of being accountable for everything—actions, situations, processes. This, too, can go to an extreme: worry, anxiety, and hypertension can result, along with obnoxious oversight. These individuals have a sense of responsibility and control that comes from commitment and expectation. Confronting and managing stress and challenges can be overwhelming and eventually dysfunctional if they become, to use a colloquial term, "control freaks."

Each individual must eventually define and recognize who they are— what they believe in and what they stand for. They must grapple with finding out what they hope to become and contribute. Ultimately, it is simply their own responsibility: it cannot be dodged or deflected. Others certainly can influence, but the conclusive choice is their own.

ETHICS AND VICTIM MENTALITY

What do ethics have to do with children and victim mentality? Quite a lot actually. After all, helping children develop character and maturely use their increasing autonomy requires an understanding of ethical principles. Adults have a duty to help children learn principles and values to act in trustworthy and ethical ways.

Ethics "provides a set of standards that help us decide how to act in a range of situations."[3] Children must understand that their decisions affect how they live independently and with others. They need to learn that ethical principles provide more direction and questions about actions and decisions related to the basic values of justice, goodness, liberty, and equality.

As history has demonstrated, issues of right and wrong are not always easily discerned. Children realize this as they work their way through school and through their interactions with peers and others. Discovering right from wrong is not always easily discerned—there are conflicts and situations that can blur the distinctions.

Ethical conduct and decisions concern human virtues. In other words, "a person of good character would be one who attained certain virtues."[4] Living life based on meeting explicit virtues and standards results in a life of integrity and moral authority.

Children have a duty and obligation to do the right thing. In addition, the expectation is that they act with character and live the qualities and traits that it requires. Duties and virtues are the focus for children to make decisions, act to help others, and develop their abilities and contribute beyond their own self-interest. In doing so, children must consider the following questions:

- What kind of person should I be or try to be?
- What are my obligations in the situation and what are the things I should never do?

These questions focus on two things children must consider confronting circumstances: doing the right thing and acting honorably. Life presents dilemmas and ethical questions. Assuming a victim mentality does not ease or embrace those questions. In fact, assuming this mentality itself has ethical questions and implications for the individual and others.

SELF-EFFICACY

Self-efficacy concerns "a person's belief that he can perform a particular behavior that will produce a particular outcome."[5] Individuals who believe in their ability to affect outcomes have an internal locus of control. Persistence is based on the attitude that they can make a difference—an internal affirmation and confidence to act and press on.

Persistence to pursue a calling or purpose is enhanced by self-efficacy from which a sense of empowerment is formed. A sense of efficacy creates self-awareness and the ability to address issues and work with others to resolve them. Without a sense of efficacy, making positive connections to others or moving forward is difficult. Feeling empowered to persevere when faced with the possibility of rejection or failure creates the will and courage to confront adverse situations. A sense of efficacy is necessary to commit talent and ability to important issues and problem solve.

Cursing the darkness of adversity is counterproductive. There is a sweet spot in taking action. New doors open that initiate learning and different perspectives. Creativity can bloom from trials as subtle nuances and forces are discovered through diligence and confidence that can alter outcomes.

Growth is not painless or risk free, particularly if old mindsets and ways of thinking are dominant. Discomfort and frustration are a part of growing and improving.

Efficacy requires self-regulation: the ability to control responses, emotions, impulses, and thoughts in order to reach goals with integrity to ideals and standards. Self-discipline is required to do things that one may not want to do or that may be difficult. They must resist the temptation to withdraw. Self-control is related positively to students getting higher grades, fewer discipline problems, as well as the ability to adjust to circumstances.

In a contrary vein, research shows that individuals, like those demonstrating a victim mentality, self-handicap themselves by placing barriers in the way of their success as a means to protect or enhance their self-esteem or the opinion others have of them.[6] As a result, persistence goes by the wayside and eliminates the adeptness to follow through, thereby creating a built-in excuse for failure.

CHOICE AND RESPONSIBILITY

Choice theory explains, "For all practical purposes, we choose everything we do, including the misery we feel."[7] Individuals choose their thoughts and actions and how they respond. They decide whether or not to adopt a victim mentality and blame, badger, complain, and withdraw—all self-destructive behavior—or they decide to tackle an issue, become a "player," and persist.

Glasser states that these disruptive behaviors must be replaced by choosing to care, listen, support, encourage, trust, accept, love, and welcome.[8] In essence, everyone chooses how to think, how to act, and how to feel. They decide whether to actively set goals, face circumstances, and take action and make adjustments if need be. All of which affects their physiology—heartbeat, breathing, and brain function—as well as their psychological disposition and attitude.

No one can totally control the behavior, feelings, or thinking of others. By choosing to become a victim, individuals surrender their freedom of choice. "Freedom is one of our great longings—freedom to be who we must be, freedom to pursue our purpose, freedom to connect with the world in our own significant way, and freedom to create and to apply our talents and our heartfelt energy. The freedom to be oneself."[9]

In circumstances or crises, information is the only thing people can get from others. How they deal with it and act on the information is their individual choice. For example, a teacher can provide knowledge or data, but the teacher cannot do the work for the student to master it. That is also true for adults. Evaluating information and determining how it affects decisions and approaches and what to do with it is up to each individual person.

In all of this, how children think and feel about themselves is critically important. Finding contentment and joy in life depends on how they interpret experiences and events. Hapless victims filter experiences through a dark lens. If they think they can engage the challenge, then they become an active player in determining outcomes.

Stress is a factor in life. Some is self-inflicted, but it also comes from external sources beyond an individual's direct control. Some of these situations are very difficult. The issue is how they deal with the conditions and misfortune.

According to Csikszentmihalyi, some individuals have an "autotelic self."[10] These individuals confront misfortune and make something good out of it. They confront great hardships and overcome them, standing firm for their beliefs and courageously facing the state of affairs and possible opposition. Individuals actively translate potential threats into challenges and maintain an inner harmony. They are actively involved with what is transpiring.

Autotelic people set goals and make choices to achieve them; they become immersed and committed to the activity, concentrate, and focus on what is happening. They sustain involvement and learn to enjoy the experience even though it may be exhausting. All of this takes determination and discipline and can stimulate individuals to creativity and achievement. Persisting despite ups and downs of working to achieve goals and resolve issues is necessary because significant things do not always come easy.

RESILIENCE

Resilience is critically important. Many heroic stories of individuals who faced difficulty and moved ahead in life despite the trauma are based on resilience. George Vaillant defines resilience as "nothing more than the application of intelligence, streetsmarts, planfulness, and education."[11] Mature individuals realize that others have suffered worse and that things are relative to each person—their values and life experience.

Vaillant also identifies the attributes resilient youth have over their less resilient peers. Resilient youth are "humorous, emotionally responsive, nurturant, idealistic (in other words altruistic); ability to focus attention and control impulses (stoicism and suppression); enterprising and resourceful (creative) and ability to plan (anticipation)."[12] Resilient youth do not turn against themselves but move ahead and make progress.

Victim thinking and negative emotions slow or hinder resilience. Fear, anger, helplessness, and hopelessness decrease the ability to approach and solve problems and weaken resiliency. Getting "stuck in the victim/blaming mode" causes people to "reject all suggestions on how to cope with what happened."[13]

Resilient people manage their feelings in healthy ways. While they may feel grief, anger, and confusion, they don't let those feelings overwhelm them and become a permanent state. They change the way they work and approach life and make adjustments: holding up under pressure and realizing that their situation should not be under the control of others. Personal responsibility for addressing and responding to struggles and difficulty is characteristic of adaptable people.

Resilience is easier when facing events that were experienced before, particularly if individuals have a strong sense of self. Understanding and insight into values and personal history affects and determines how people confront situations. Self-esteem and self-efficacy are important foundations for resilience and commitment. Resilient individuals learn lessons that can be powerful and life changing.

CHANGING MINDSETS

Facing the pain of defeat or loss takes courage, which is necessary to overcome a counterproductive victim mindset. Confronting negativism involves self-awareness and recognizing and understanding one's feelings and thoughts.

In the book *The Power of Resilience*, Brooks and Goldstein state, "Self-awareness means having a deep understanding of one's emotions, as well as one's strengths and limitations and one's values and motives. People with strong self-awareness are realistic—neither overly self-critical nor naïvely hopeful. Rather they are honest with themselves about themselves."[14]

Self-aware people have the distinction of being self-reflective, thinking things over, and avoiding being impulsive. Kofman states that self-awareness allows us to "not only perceive the external world, we can also bear witness to our internal world. We can pose questions like, 'Why am I thinking what I am thinking?' 'Do I have sound reasons for my conclusions?' Am I letting my desires cloud my judgment?'"[15]

Resilience is very important for children. In fact, it is critical for them because they have to learn how to respond to situations that include stress, pressure, and challenge. In the process of growing up, children confront many things, some unpleasant, for the first time. Coping and bouncing back from disappointments, failures, and frustrations is necessary to grow and fulfill their promise.

First of all, children must recognize the issues they face—not deny them. Helping children focus on their strengths is part of problem solving. The presence of an adult who believes in them is powerful in helping them address issues.

Brooks and Goldstein assert that resilient children successfully address issues if they have the following mindset qualities: a sense of feeling appreciated and the ability to set realistic expectations and goals for themselves.[16] They make decisions and see setbacks as challenges and are aware of their weaknesses and strengths. Finally, they develop effective interpersonal skills and are able to define the aspects of their lives they can control and focus their energy on them.

Aptitude is not always a guarantee of victory and achievement. Passion and perseverance are key ingredients, at times, that make a critical difference. Things do not always unfold based on an individual's preference or schedule. Competition or predicaments, as well as criticism, can be stronger and more severe than expected.

The underdog Olympic hockey team applied themselves and had the grit to face a more talented and accomplished opponent and defeat them in a high-stress situation. It was called a "miracle" on ice. But was it, really? Or was it the result of a mindset of endurance, commitment, and dedication? Tenacity can be learned. Miracles are not miracles if they can be achieved by strength of will, pride, and determination. They are made by perseverance, agility, and passion—all important things individuals can control and influence.

One misstep should not deter children from persisting. Carrying on and not giving up takes grit and determination and requires practice, purpose, and hope. Enjoying the challenge is an asset because it results in enthusiasm. Having a daily discipline to improve requires practice. Believing in mission and work results in purpose. Finally, hope is rising to the occasion and is involved in facing difficulty and doubts. When individuals do this, they can be masters of their fate, not victims without options.

Defining what is and what isn't controllable is necessary. Pursuing those things that can be controlled or influenced through sound decision-making is the key to reasonable action and may affect those circumstances beyond direct control. Focusing on anger and frustration only weakens an individual's efforts.

A critical part of the journey of life with meaning and happiness requires truth and wisdom. M. Scott Peck states that life is "continuous and stringent self-examination. We know the world through our relationship to it. . . . The life of wisdom must be a life of contemplation combined with action."[17]

POINTS TO REMEMBER

- Success sometimes is born from failure.
- People can be smart but not wise.

- "Being" and "doing" are both important in life. People do things, but they are human "beings" that direct their doings.
- Ethics set standards for behavior, choices, and decisions.
- Self-efficacy is the personal belief that an individual can act in ways to produce desired outcomes.
- Self-efficacy is related to self-regulation and self-control. Individuals choose how to think, how they feel, and how they act with the autonomy at their disposal.
- Individuals have an autotelic self: they confront hardships and misfortune and overcome by standing for beliefs and maintaining a sense of inner harmony. They set goals and plans to achieve results.
- Obligations are of a higher moral standard than responsibilities.
- Maturity requires competence, understanding, judgment, and accountability.
- Being proactive requires analyzing, determining forces and feelings, defining possibilities, and acting on those things that can be addressed or influenced.
- Resilience is nothing more than applying intelligence, streetsmarts, and education.
- Self-awareness includes being self-reflective, understanding one's emotions, and realistically understanding stress and weaknesses.
- Resilient children have a sense of self-awareness.

NOTES

1. George A. Goens, *Soft Leadership for Hard Times* (Lanham, MD: Rowman & Littlefield, 2005), 48.
2. Richard Parncutt, "Victim Mentality, Self-Efficacy, and Politics," September 2015, http://www.parncutt.org/victim.html.
3. Sheila Bonde and Paul Firenza, "A Framework for Making Ethical Decisions," Brown University, May, 2013, https://www.brown.edu/academics/science-and-technology-studies/sites/brown.edu.academics.science-and-technology-studies/files/uploads/Framework.pdf.
4. Ibid.
5. Christopher Peterson, Steven F. Maier, and Martin E. P. Seligman, *Learned Helplessness* (New York: Oxford University Press, 1993), 228–29.
6. Christopher Peterson and Martin E. P. Seligman, *Character Strengths and Virtues* (New York: Oxford University Press, 2004), 233.
7. William Glasser, *Choice Theory: A New Psychology for Personal Freedom* (New York: HarperCollins, 2010), Kindle edition, 3.
8. Ibid., 21.
9. Goens, *Soft Leadership for Hard Times*, 85.
10. Mihaly Csikszentmihalyi, *Flow* (New York: HarperCollins, 2008), Kindle edition, 200.
11. George Vaillant, *The Wisdom of the Ego* (Cambridge, MA: Harvard University Press, 1993), 305.
12. Ibid., 288.
13. Al Siebert, *The Resiliency Advantage* (San Francisco: Barrett-Koehler, 2005), 2–4.

14. Robert Brooks and Sam Goldstein, *The Power of Resilience: Achieving Balance, Confidence and Personal Strength in Your Life* (New York: McGraw-Hill Education, 2004), Kindle edition, loc. 2713.

15. Kofman, *Conscious Business: How to Build Value through Values* (Boulder, CO: Sounds True, 2006) 3.

16. Robert Brooks and Sam Goldstein, *Raising Resilient Children* (New York: McGraw Hill, 2001), Kindle edition, loc. 197–200.

17. M. Scott Peck, *The Road Less Traveled* (New York: Simon & Schuster, 1978), 51.

Chapter Seven

Teachers, Schools, and Responsibility

"The aim [of education] must be the training of independently acting and thinking individuals who, however, see in the service to the community their highest life achievement." —Albert Einstein

"Far better it is to dare mighty things, to win glorious triumphs, even though checkered by failure, than to take rank with those poor spirits who neither enjoy much nor suffer much, because they live in the gray twilight that knows neither victory nor defeat." —Theodore Roosevelt

Historically, public education has been the foundation for the development of our children and cultivation of our society. In many cases, the American Dream is given birth in classrooms every day for students. Children's imagination and enthusiasm to seek knowledge, investigate ideas, and embrace personal development are the intangible gifts that come from a quality education and the relationship between teacher and student. The resulting motivation not only provides satisfaction to the individual, but over time is the seed that produces creative and energizing ideas and solutions to problems and issues.

Quality education is important to all of us. Unfortunately, we reduce the purpose of education to simply getting into a college or gaining employment. But it is more than that, and too often we have failed to define what it means to be well-educated.

Thomas Friedman states, "Education, whether it comes from parents or schools, has to be about more than just cognitive skills. It also has to include character building. The fact is, parents and schools and cultures can and do shape people."[1] The world is changing, and children will have to adjust and accommodate with the times. An education for today will be obsolete tomorrow if we only emphasize jobs and technical skills.

What the future holds is uncertain, but change is inevitable, and children will need to confront a future requiring more than the recall and recitation of facts. Anyone over fifty years old today can testify to the fact that conditions are vastly different than thirty years ago concerning employment, technology, and social and political matters. Education must be dynamic and ongoing, emphasizing the principles and values that form the foundation of our democracy and society.

As a nation, individuals are encouraged to follow their bliss and aspirations. Public schools are vital resources to enable each individual to have the ability and perspective to engage in that pursuit.

Happiness and meaning require an education that extends beyond content mastery to ethical understanding, divergent thinking, and cultivating wisdom. In actuality, the real search is for an individual to discover who they are—their talents, passion, and path in life.

In this process of self-discovery, they will unlock their uniqueness and understand their connections to the world, society, and family. A good education helps children recognize what wants to emerge from within them and possibilities for the future.

Children and adults need to open their minds with a fresh perspective and to perceive what is unfolding in the world. They must be mindful and aware of the integration of issues and ideas and what is evolving. An open mind and heart involve the intersection of understanding obligations to others and themselves, and in order to do that, empathy, honesty, and compassion are important.

Education must move beyond standardization and rigidity to creative environments and teaching. In an unfolding world, creativity and the continuous intellectual curiosity to respond and shape the future are required. Understanding obligations in a democratic society and gaining a sense of historical perspective about duty to family, community, and country are cornerstones to the way of life in our society.

However, the current straitjacket of overregulation and mandates inhibits creativity and intellectual curiosity in schools. Mandated educational policies like high-stakes testing and false metrical standards guarantee that teachers will not be able to establish an environment that allows children to experience and explore deeper levels of awareness, creativity, and comprehension.

Change is the consequence of inspiration, conflict, and innovation. Intellectual skills are more than literacy and numeracy. They involve: attaining information and organizing it, defining the values that undergird arguments, articulating ideas clearly, formulating new viewpoints, and questioning assumptions and theories. Being able to analyze, synthesize, and evaluate issues, concepts, and information is vital.

Problem solving involves a broad perspective across content and a deep understanding of principles and moral expectations. Comprehension of cultural values and their philosophical foundations is required for ethical decision making and moral conduct to create and maintain a civil society.

IMPENDING CHANGES

Social, political, and technological disruptions occur in life. It's called progress, and everyone is going to experience it. On a broad level, the impact of technological change has affected almost every facet of daily life. Dramatic transformations have taken place as new perspectives and legal precedents have evolved. The effects of a changing economy, from a manufacturing to one of finance along with greater international competition and investment, have altered corporate and economic growth as well as employment.

Children will face similar, if not greater, changes in their lives. Consequently, they have to have the character, educational, ethical, and intellectual skills to contribute and adapt to the innovations and changes that will come. Even today, there is an understanding that the skills people need to thrive in the future are different than what is required now. Skills alone, however, do not provide the understanding necessary to thrive in shifting times.

A report written by the World Economic Forum compares the skills needed today to what will be required in 2020.[2] The report identifies the top ten skills necessary because of the impact of artificial intelligence, biotechnology, autonomous transport, advanced robotics, and genomics. The ranked comparisons of skills in 2015 to those needed in 2020 are included in the table below.

Creativity is the skill that will change the most from 2015 to 2020, becoming one of the top three skills individuals will need because of new products, new technologies, and new ways of working. Creativity is essential

Table 7.1. Required Skills Comparison

Required Skills—2015	Required Skills—2020
1. Complex problem solving	1. Complex problem solving
2. Coordinating with others	2. Critical thinking
3. People management	3. Creativity
4. Critical thinking	4. People management
5. Negotiation	5. Coordinating with others
6. Quality control	6. Emotional intelligence
7. Service orientation	7. Judgment and decision making
8. Judgment and decision making	8. Service orientation
9. Active listening	9. Negotiations
10. Creativity	10. Cognitive flexibility

to apply technologies to production and the workplace, as well as discover new approaches and methods to gain the most benefit from the changes.

The impact of artificial intelligence will affect the analysis of data and lower-level decision making. With the transformation of the economy, students will have to apply higher-order thinking skills, creativity, and innovation, as well as apply the principles and values that undergird society in changing times. Character is a major quality that is necessary to respond to those technological, social, and economic changes. Companies and enterprises do not have time to deal with excuse mongers and blamers.

STUDENTS AND SCHOOL

Students are like every other person on the planet. No two are the same. They do not look for the same things in life or have the same ambitions and talents. Perspectives are not the same. They are also in the process of growing and maturing, and physical and emotional development move at different rates, as do their priorities. Their family background, philosophy, functionality, and support are varied and divergent. Some look forward to school, and for others it is not a top priority.

As teachers can attest, students exhibit a spectrum of behavior and attitudes toward education and learning.[3] Some of these characteristics are highly productive while some are very detrimental to teaching and learning. Dysfunctional behavior, in fact, can be outwardly hostile and uncooperative, or it can be exhibited passively yet aggressively.

Teachers sometimes project what their students will be like in the future. Some are projected to be wonderful musicians, community officials, or business leaders. Then there are others: the class clown who at times can bring laughter but also disruptive irritation or the serious, highly introverted academic student who can be enthused only by working alone on technology apps. Then there's Bruce.

In the upper grades and high school, many teachers didn't project success for him. He was the kid who had to give a speech to the entire class about something of interest to him. Bruce stood up, pulled out a cigarette and a book of matches, lit it, and proceeded to give a talk about "how to smoke." He certainly got attention and a reputation along with castigation from the teacher.

He got in fights, hung with the wrong guys, and was drinking beer and smoking at the age of thirteen. Sometimes in those fights he was defending himself, and other times he bullied other kids.

Being sent to the vice principal's office was not a unique experience for him. And, yes, he had excuses for his behavior with which he plied teachers and the principal that certainly would not pass muster in a lie detector test. Of course, he had excuses and blamed others or circumstances for his plight.

To be sure, some teachers thought that Bruce, the troublemaker, was destined for problems as a teen and even worse as an adult. He drank too much in his late teens and early twenties, got into a few fights, and even tried to outrun the police on his motorcycle, which caused him to spend a few nights in jail.

Bruce had issues. He built walls and kept people out. Life wasn't easy for him—he was reacting to a world he didn't like. His father died suddenly when he was nine years old, and he was one of nine children raised by his mother after his dad's death. Life for a widow working and raising nine children is not an easy role under any circumstances.

But Bruce made it! No, he didn't find a cure for cancer or become a famous rock 'n' roller (although he does karaoke occasionally), but he has been successful, which might be a big surprise to some of his former teachers.

His father was strict and remained a presence in his life even after he died when Bruce was so young. He didn't let Bruce off the hook, and he wouldn't give Bruce the answers. He had him reflect on his behavior and outcomes and think it through.

Teachers made a positive impression on him by holding him accountable in a caring way. Mrs. Swanton, his seventh grade math teacher, would have him sit in the hallway when he was disruptive but then spent her lunch hour with Bruce going over the day's lesson. Today, he would like to thank her for her dedication and care.

Bruce met Linda who helped change his mindset. They got married, and he stopped fighting and curtailed drinking because he realized the importance of her in his life. He realized that he had to tear down the walls, be open to others, and consciously decide to change his life and "be there for his wife and children."

The trek for Bruce was no piece of cake. Teachers and others cannot always see the impact they have on children. Sometimes the lessons they impart are experienced but take a long time to reveal their impact. Introspection does not occur overnight but is a product of many events and the influence of people.

The fact that people care, provide direction and discipline, and communicate positive values can over time help children grow into responsible and response-able adults. Walls come down and self-victimization stops and life and success happen.

Certainly, the vast majority of students are cooperative and responsive in their own way and to a variety of degrees. Academic ability, generally, is the meter to gauge children's success and adaptability to school. As with everything else in growing to maturity, fully developing and utilizing one's talents and aptitudes takes time and experience. Mentors and role models play a consequential and indispensable role.

Teachers use various verbs and phrases to describe students. Reading the comments in e-mails and report cards also provides descriptions of children. In one case, "easily distracted" and "ants in his pants" were phrases a mother back in the 1950s responded to in some correspondence with the third grade teacher. While a bit vernacular, the comments clearly expressed the issue free of any pseudo-scientific terminology or technical acronyms. The mother responded clearly and indicated what she would do at home to solve the "ants" problem and encourage better focus in class.

Functional students are frequently described as hard workers and organized, driven to excel, and focused on results and achievement. These students follow rules and are attentive in meeting expectations.

Other students, while not disruptive in class, exhibit more challenging, independent styles and raise issues and push the boundaries of education. Conversely, there are students who are accommodating and focus on the point of view of others. They go along even if it sometimes denies their own wants and opinions.

Creative students may be less concerned with the attitude of others but are proud of their uniqueness and expressiveness: they have flair and like self-expression and enjoy lessons that spur their interests. Because of their creative arc and poise, they are sometimes overly sensitive to criticism.

Other students have active minds but prefer solitude away from groups and social activities. They are thoughtful and responsive, but social effectiveness or acceptance does not drive their interests. Reserved and quiet, they enjoy the discussion of ideas.

Still other students are "people pleasing" or want to be recognized as the "star" of the class. The "cheerleader" types bound with energy, enthusiasm, and social flair. Sociability and popularity are important to them—social status is the goal.

What motivates students differs and is a driving force behind their behavior and effort. The support of teachers is often a turning point in children's perception of themselves. "When the world around us supports and reinforces our motivation, a strong tailwind aligns with all our energy, propelling us strongly toward our aspirations."[4]

Teachers establish a culture and climate in their classroom to help and motivate students. But not all classroom climates and cultures are the same because teachers, too, have different perspectives and personalities and interpretations of education. A student may function productively in one classroom and exhibit to different degrees distracting, disturbing, or disrespectful behavior in others.

Teachers experience strong attention-seeking behavior by some students who want to be heard and recognized, dominating discussions or activities and often curtailing other students' input and recognition. On the other side of the ledger are inattentive students who drift off in their own thoughts or talk to neighboring students, diverting both of them from the task at hand.

Coming unprepared for class—not completing assignments or not bringing materials—is very disruptive to the individual and the entire class. Time is wasted, class focus distracted, and activities compromised.

Reasons for unpreparedness run the gamut: fear of failure, not understanding the assignment, disinterest, irresponsibility, dysfunctional home life, or others. In any event, the classroom is thrown off course and students are restricted from active engagement.

Finally, lack of civility is a major disturbance for both teachers and students in class. Time is lost as the behavior disrupts the thoughts of students, is disrespectful to teachers, and, at times, explodes into physical confrontation.

SCHOOL, STUDENTS, AND VICTIM MENTALITY

Students with a victim mentality are disruptive in their own way. Though they may be very capable academically and skilled and talented, their beliefs about themselves compromise their performance and affiliation with others. They are self-destructive and exhausting to themselves and to others, including teachers. The sad thing is they learned and adopted this behavior from the example of others: it is not a psychological malady.

First, they have very limiting beliefs about themselves—the inability to influence or own the situation or circumstances they are in. Powerlessness is the attitude that can be discerned from their words: "I can't . . . ," "I don't know . . . ," "Not my fault. . . ." Their refusal or perceived inability to see choices cements them in their circumstances. In some respects, they fear the risk of acting and the possibility of falling short.

Second, students with a victim mentality perceive negative intentions in other people—students, teachers, parents, and others. In some cases, they see other students as luckier than themselves and certainly happier and sometimes a threat to their self-image. Jealousy of others' achievements can initiate alibis or defamatory remarks. They view situations, some of their own making, and ask "Why me?"

Finally, they refuse to accept any responsibility for their behavior, circumstances, or outcomes. Outcomes and results are attributed to external sources and deny the concept of hard work. Why try? If they don't try, then in their minds they don't fail. They focus on the negative, make excuses, use deceit and lies to avoid responsibility, and wallow in problems feeling sorry for themselves. Accountability, an important obligation, is avoided and rejected.

These students miss opportunities because of fearing failure or the need to maintain and protect a self-concept by making excuses, using "put-downs," or refusing to engage. Listening to other points of view is rejected, as is a sense of responsibility for others.

Blaming is related to character. Tartaglia indicates why people blame:[5]

- Blame and resentment is fear of accountability.
- Blame is a good way to take the heat off yourself.
- Blaming others is a way of maintaining self-esteem and looking good in the eyes of others.
- Blame and resentment is a character flaw that splits people into good and bad groups and helps the blamer cope with a "hostile world."

Students with a victim mentality seek sympathy, create drama, and destroy relationships. Unfortunately, they engage in self-destructive behavior and limit their experiences, restrict sharpening their abilities, and eventually isolate themselves from others. Passive-aggression is a familiar strategy used at home and school.

SCHOOLS AND CHARACTER DEVELOPMENT

Character undergirds behavior and the decisions individuals make. This is certainly apparent at school as children are formulating and testing their character through their experiences and observations. Character is the "psychological muscles that allow a person to control impulses and defer gratification, which is essential for achievement, performance, and moral conduct."[6]

Success requires more than cognitive effort. Impulse control, self-motivation, and the ability to confront and overcome stress are important. Parents send their children to school not only for academics, but also for discipline and character development. Eventually, they will require developing self-discipline—the ability to commit and mobilize and to confront challenges and meet goals and aspirations.

Actions and behavior, however, must be based on positive values. Schools are value-focused organizations, with cultures and climates. These cultures are critical in teaching and learning appropriate behavior and in holding students accountable. "Trying to develop character without attention to sharing values with the young is like trying to develop the muscles of an athlete without having a particular sport in mind."[7]

Commitment to principles and values is essential in personal decisions, social circumstances, work context, and political responsibilities. Children learn by experience and reflection more than through lectures.

Children will face a multitude of experiences, emotions, people, and situations over their lifetime. The stability of core values and strength of character to lead a stable, well-lived life requires doing the right thing at the right time in all circumstances. Specific strengths are required: kindness, social intelligence, self-control, hope, and perspective buffer against the negative effects of stress, trauma, uncertainty, and their associated problems.[8]

Peterson and Seligman define the character strengths needed throughout life that students should learn.[9] They classified the strengths into the following areas:

- *Wisdom and Knowledge:* cognitive strengths requiring gaining and applying knowledge; including creativity, curiosity, open-mindedness, critical thinking, love of learning, and perspective and wisdom.
- *Courage:* emotional strength and the will to accomplish goals in the face of internal and external opposition: bravery, persistence, integrity, honesty and authenticity, vitality, vigor and enthusiasm.
- *Justice:* civic strength that supports a healthy community life: citizenship, social responsibility, loyalty, fairness, leadership.
- *Temperance:* strengths that protect against excess: forgiveness and mercy, humility and modesty, prudence and self-regulation.
- *Transcendence:* strengths form connection to a larger universe and meaning: appreciation of beauty and excellence, gratitude, hope and optimism, fair-mindedness, humor, and spirituality.

These character strengths require study, exploration, and the support of teachers and parents and should be the foundation for the school's culture. Persistence and consistency are necessary in school and life. Self-regulation is a marker of maturity and wisdom in all relationships and activities.

Wisdom is not simply an esoteric or philosophical concept and is more than cleverness. "Wisdom . . . is more than intelligence. It suggests a special quality of judgment in human affairs based on knowledge of moral principles, human nature, human needs, and human values. Wisdom is more than what people know, it is who they have become; and who they have become is determined by how congruent their behavior is with their knowledge. It is not enough for leaders to know moral principles—to have credibility as leaders and thus to earn followership, they must live up to their knowledge."[10]

Park and Peterson indicate that schools need to teach specific activities to help develop character strengths and encourage children to use them in their daily lives. "Saying 'do your best' or 'be the best you can be' is not a good way to cultivate character. Young people need to be instructed to choose the target strengths on which they want to focus, to set specific and measurable goals, and devise concrete action plans to achieve these goals."[11] Long-term vision and commitment, coupled with hard work and endurance, are positive traits that produce satisfaction even if the goal was not attained or attainable.

While character certainly demands effort and persistence, it also includes courage to venture into new territory, creativity, open-mindedness to new ideas, and not being attached to the past or predetermined outcomes. Being helpless is hapless: wisdom seeks options and the application of different thinking and frames of mind to move ahead.

Teachers must focus on helping students move to a growth mindset that encourages children for their efforts and processes: in other words, their intentions and actions. The process of learning is facing challenges and is more akin to the real work of scientists or artists. In innovative businesses, too, failure is a part of creativity and productivity if there is a process to accept it, analyze it, and recharge it. "We should promote the kind of accountability in which students must show they have mastered subject matter, but also can think analytically, creatively, and practically with it."[12]

Success has to do with maturity and self-understanding. Intelligence and judgment and principled behavior are intrinsic to successful adults. In addition to academics, schools and teachers deal with social, psychoemotional, and moral and ethical issues, as well as judgment and relationships.

When reformers look at teachers, they frequently reduce them to data results and purveyors of "best practices." Sometimes they see a teacher's work as mechanical, scripted, and procedure oriented: a viewpoint that ignores the human element in learning.

The biggest role teachers play is as polestars—significant people who create deep connections and mentor and nurture children so that they can be their best. Often, this entails telling them in a caring way the difficult truths that they need to hear in order to be the person they desire to be. This may include feedback not only on their classwork, but also about their attitudes, behavior, perspectives, and physical development. This isn't simply patting them on the head and praising them, but giving them feedback that causes them to self-reflect about their behavior, attitude, and approaches.

Research shows a positive relationship with an adult who provides support is a critical factor in helping children. "Some children need help overcoming feelings of isolation and support in developing connections to others. Effective schools make sure that opportunities exist for adults to spend quality, personal time with children. Effective schools also foster positive student interpersonal relations—they encourage students to help each other and to feel comfortable assisting others in getting help when needed."[13]

People have had defining moments with teachers, principals, coaches, and others. Such moments stay with individuals throughout life and continue to be helpful beacons in frustrating and difficult times.

Defining moments and polestars encourage people to look at what's under the surface and get a clear perspective of circumstances and options. A truthful and caring moment can clarify perspective and implications and bring about understanding and change.

"They may surface something hidden. They can crystallize what was fluid and unformed. They may give a sharp, clear view of something previously obscure. In every case, however, a defining moment reveals something important about a person's basic values and about his or her abiding commitments in life."[14]

The future can seem ominous to children, and for those huddled in the victim crouch, it can seem impossible. But everyone has to find their way and choose to realize the goals most important to them. Help may be present, but individuals must be ready to receive it. Significance cannot be imposed; it is the result of a relationship that is perceived as "helping."

ACTIVE LISTENING

One essential tool in helping relationships is active listening, which includes listening carefully to the content and intent of the message. Active listening increases the ability to better comprehend the message rather than immediately disagreeing, dismissing, or ignoring it. This process demonstrates respect for the individual and is usually reciprocated.

Frequently, the lack of listening creates breaches in relationships, misunderstandings, and disrespect because minds become cast in stone, attention is diverted, or no effort is made to understand or comprehend differing opinions. Sometimes it's just a matter of not really caring.

Listening is a fundamental skill that is frequently taken for granted or not practiced seriously. Actually, it is fundamental in every aspect of our lives. We hear the problem when people say, "My wife doesn't understand what I'm saying," "I don't get it; I told him what to do," or "You never listen to me—you just see the words flow from my mouth."

Too often a phrase from the movie *Cool Hand Luke*, "What we got here is a failure to communicate," is an accurate reflection. People blame communication if things do not go their way, as a frequent excuse and avoidance of consequences for failure.

What is necessary is for children and adults to listen actively—for the content and intent of messages. Basically, that means to actively seek understanding, accuracy, and clarity, which requires not talking over someone or performing rebuttals before people are finished expressing their thoughts. Repeating the message in one's own words to see if the interpretation is accurate is important. And, finally, listening with an open mind and fully exchanging ideas and perceptions are essential.

Understanding requires hearing the content and comprehending the intention and the attitude behind it. People generally can comprehend content—the meaning of the words and sentences. The major issue is the intent of the message. At times, the intent of the content is sarcasm (e.g., saying "Good job!" to someone could sarcastically mean "You really blew it!"). Understanding the content and intent of communications is essential. Today, with Twitter and text messages, making that distinction is not always easy.

Active listening is very important in communicating with students—understanding their perceptions and viewpoints as well as their feelings. Adults have to teach them to listen actively, too, so they comprehend the expressed position and decisions. This skill is easier said than done. It takes thought, training, patience, and respect.

SCHOOLS AND MATURITY

The foundation of maturity is the character traits discussed earlier, which take time to understand, develop, and practice. Mature adults and leaders have the following characteristics that are pertinent to all people. Bill O'Brien is an author and prominent figure in the classic business book *The Fifth Discipline*.[15] It might seem strange to quote O'Brien in a book about children, but his philosophy is geared to fully developing the people with whom he worked by building positive character. In life, character and maturity are essential to make wise choices, grow, and continue to learn.

He asserts that maturity includes:

- strong convictions guided by strong beliefs and values
- commitments flowing from beliefs and values about significant matters: family, society, and work
- openness by revealing feelings and concerns and being good listeners
- "free will" and inner strength coming from exercising freedom of choice, which includes harmony: "We believe in what we do"
- deferred gratification by choosing future rewards over short-term ones to maintain greater control of their destiny
- accurate maps that provide a clear view of reality and using information from all perspectives in making decisions and relationships
- moral courage to make tough and unpopular decisions when necessary in reaching worthwhile and ethical goals

These qualities are necessary for all mature adults. Children have to learn and grow into them by facing situations, not avoiding conflict, speaking up, and making proper choices even if it means rejection from peers. Safer and popular choices are not always the right ones, and certainly, humility is important, as is seeking wise counsel in making decisions.

Sometimes students have more choices than they think. They certainly have a choice of how they respond emotionally, which includes being positive or negative about their actions. Those who feel they are victims of circumstances and allow themselves to wallow in negativity can get stuck emotionally and let everything "get" to them. In essence, by taking everything personally, they begin to feel they have lost control of their lives to external events, people, or fate.

Helping students to get out of this mentality and stay positive and learn that they have the choice to express themselves positively is important. Being introspective can encourage students to see what they can do in class or other circumstances.

Understanding that they are responsible for their own learning—not teachers or others—can help them break through defensive and negative postures. They must learn that it is not external forces that govern their life, but it is their internal decisions and attitude that are most important in addressing issues. Their attitude plants the seeds of failure or success.

A curious offshoot of victim mentality, according to a study published in the *Journal of Personality and Social Psychology*, is that "people who have been wronged are reminded of the time they were wronged and feel entitled to positive outcomes" and follow a suffering-to-selfishness cycle.[16] This sense of entitlement is self-centered and can be dysfunctional in social or work groups and is characterized by lashing out and using guilt to make people feel obligated to help them. In life, everyone confronts situations where they feel victimized, but do not adopt a mentality that persists with the expectation of special treatment.

Children who come from difficult backgrounds can achieve success and be resilient. Finn and Rock cites that school engagement factors like coming to school and class on time, being prepared for and participating in class work, expending effort to complete assignments, and not being disruptive in class are significant factors in school success for all students.[17] These factors relate to dependability, personal discipline, and positive work habits.

Involved in gaining and applying these factors is the personal and academic support of parents and teachers that are "especially important to students at risk." In addition, smaller school class sizes can be an aspect in their success.

Children, whether from disadvantaged or privileged circumstances, need the sustained attention of adults. The assumption is sometimes made that affluent parents provide more support for their children, but in these circumstances, the aspirations of adults sometimes take precedence over the needs of their children. Long-lasting and clear relationships have a profound influence on children, who may not have that kind of support at home.

Botstein defines specific maxims that apply for teachers, parents, and other adults to help children grow and develop into maturity.[18] These include:

- Listen to children, follow their thinking, and respect their world.
- Help children figure things out for themselves and find answers. They don't need to know you have the answer: the important thing is how to arrive at the answer.
- Do not let children disparage that they do not know or understand.
- Show children that you enjoy thinking and are curious. Demonstrate a love of learning.
- Encourage children to spend time alone, particularly in adolescence. Do not let them judge themselves primarily in terms of peer perceptions or perspectives. Do not let them subordinate what they think to a peer group that is not based on adult wisdom but simply physical attributes and good looks.
- Do not make a sharp distinction between small and large matters concerning questions of right or wrong.
- Help children see beyond surfaces and appearances with a critical and receptive eye—notice what people say and how they present themselves.
- Encourage children to hear and to practice active listening: hearing the tone of voice and color of sound. Appreciating silence is good, too.
- Encourage children to write. Good readers are those who can write. After all, writing is thinking made visible.
- Connect with children through reading—they should see adults engaged in reading newspapers and books.
- Show children that you change your mind and how and why—they need to see adults connect thought and action. Give reasons for the change.
- Avoid complaining constantly in their presence—remember victim mentality is a learned behavior. Children need to see optimism.
- Cultivate a sense of humor.
- Foster a concern for the welfare of others—children learn by watching and the examples we provide are very potent.
- Teach the value and importance of holding to convictions. They should see adults follow their own path based on principles, values, and ethics.
- Stress the open-ended character of knowledge, interpretation, and inquiry. Teach them not to judge too quickly or harshly. Help them learn to make responsible judgments.
- Resist conventional wisdom by respecting tradition and authority with skepticism—questioning it is not a negative.

Finally, Botstein expresses concern over victimization as a metaphor for life. He states, "We would like to avoid taking responsibility for our lot in life. We would like to ascribe our failures and unhappiness to forces larger than ourselves: the society, the culture, the economy, our employers, our teachers, our parents. The generalization of victim status has gone well beyond its reasonable application. Children must learn that we are willing to take responsibility for our lot in life. If we take responsibility, we may be less inclined to complain, because if we do complain, then we inevitably have to blame ourselves. If we accept responsibility, we will then be more inclined to do something about that which we complain about. That, in turn, might lead to having less to complain about."[19]

Children must learn a sense of responsibility and optimism. Both are important to their education, how life unfolds, and how they face its consequences.

POINTS TO REMEMBER

- An education is more than cognitive skills and passing standardized tests. It involves character, the arts, self-understanding, and purpose.
- Creativity and intellectual curiosity respond to and shape the future, as well as increase understanding and responsibilities.
- Children will face dramatic changes in their lifetime. Education must focus on ethics, character, and critical thinking so they can adapt and direct changing circumstances.
- Students exhibit a spectrum of behavior and attitudes toward school and education. Teachers establish a culture and climate in schools to help motivate and cultivate students' abilities and ambitions.
- Students with victim identity focus on the negative, make excuses, avoid responsibility, and wallow in self-pity.
- Children need to develop the character strengths of wisdom and knowledge, courage, justice, temperance, and transcendence.
- Wisdom is not some esoteric concept: it concerns the quality of judgment based on principles and values and helps individuals live up to them in daily life.
- A major role teachers play is that of polestar: significant people who mentor and guide students through clear feedback delivered in a caring manner.
- Defining moments help individuals understand what's under the surface and get a clear perspective of circumstances and options. These moments stay with people throughout life as guideposts.
- Active listening is a critical skill in developing relationships and in working with students.

- Maturity involves positive character traits, convictions, openness to ideas, and moral courage.
- Children must learn to take responsibility for their lot in life.

NOTES

1. Thomas L. Friedman, *The World Is Flat* (New York: Farrar, Strauss, and Giroux, 2005), 305.
2. Alex Gray, "The 10 Skills You Need to Thrive in the Fourth Industrial Revolution," World Economic Forum, January 19, 2016, https://www.weforum.org/agenda/2016/01/the-10-skills-you-need-to-thrive-in-the-fourth-industrial-revolution.
3. Rob Fitzel, "The Nine Types of Students," The Enneagram, 2001, http://www.fitzel.ca/enneagram/education/index.html.
4. Richard Parncutt, "Victim Mentality, Self-Efficacy, and Politics," September 2015, http://www.parncutt.org/victim.html.
5. Louis A. Tartaglia, *Flawless* (New York: William Morrow and Company, 1999), 62.
6. Amitai Etzioni, *The Spirit of Community* (New York: Crown, 1993), 91.
7. Ibid., 95.
8. Nansook Park and Christopher Peterson, "Character Strengths: Research and Practice," *Journal of College and Character* 10, no. 4 (April 2009).
9. Christopher Peterson and Martin E. P. Seligman, *Character Strengths and Virtues* (New York: Oxford University Press, 2004), 29–30.
10. William J. O'Brien, *Character at Work* (New York: Paulist Press, 2008), 96.
11. Park and Peterson, "Character Strengths: Research and Practice," 7.
12. Robert J. Sternberg, "Creativity Is a Habit," *Education Week*, February 21, 2006, http://www.edweek.org/ew/articles/2006/02/22/24sternberg.h25.html.
13. Robert Brooks and Sam Goldstein, *The Power of Resilience: Achieving Balance, Confidence, and Personal Strength in Your Life* (New York: McGraw-Hill Education, 2004), Kindle edition, loc. 3026.
14. Joseph L. Badaracco, *Defining Moments* (Boston: Harvard Business School Press, 1997), 57.
15. O'Brien, *Character at Work*, 117–22.
16. Emily M. Zitek, Alexander H. Jordan, Benoit Monin, and Frederick R. Leach, "Victim Entitlement to Behave Selfishly," *Journal of Personality and Social Psychology* 98, no. 2 (2010): 245–55.
17. Jeremy D. Finn and Donald A. Rock, "Academic Success among Students at Risk for School Failure," *Journal of Applied Psychology* 82, no. 2 (1997), 231.
18. Leon Botstein, *Jefferson's Children* (New York: Doubleday, 1997), 134–35.
19. Ibid., 168–69.

Chapter Eight

Parents, Children, and Responsibility

"Parents have such incredible power to confirm and influence the inner life of the child. Identity is fashioned in the inner life. The child's sensibility is like a sponge. It absorbs everything. Without knowing it, we drink in the voices of our parents at that stage. We have not yet developed any kind of filter to sift the creative from the destructive.

"The memory of childhood is so rich that it takes a lifetime to unpack. Again and again, we remember certain scenes, not always the most dramatic, and gradually come to a kind of self-understanding and an understanding of our parents." —John O'Donohue

"The surest way to make your child unhappy is to accustom him to get everything he wants." —Jean-Jacques Rousseau

All new parents look with amazement, joy, and optimism at the birth of an infant and the miracle of a new life. The aspiration of parenthood transforms into the dream of a promising future for this new person. Hope. Happiness. Success. Love. Fulfillment.

Most parents would agree with Jefferson's statement that this child "would be free to make himself all he was capable of becoming."[1] All parents hope for a rewarding life for their children. They have a formative role in helping their child get off to a positive start and develop the attitudes and character to do so.

In fact, parenting is one of the most important roles a person can undertake. Parenting, however, has changed. According to the Pew Research Center in their report on the American family, there has been a decline over the past fifty years in the percent of children living in two-parent households: from 87 percent in 1960 to 69 percent today.[2]

Parents are now raising children within a context of greater diversity and nontraditional family forms: from two parents to a single parent, from marital to nonmarital cohabitation, and from biological to blended families. In addition, the percentage of children born outside of marriage has increased to 71 percent and 53 percent in black and Hispanic families, respectively.

The Pew research also cites examples of how the financial status of parents impacts their ability to provide for their children. For example, access to a safe neighborhood environment is more limited for children of lower-income parents than it is for their more affluent counterparts. Parental income also affects children's opportunities to participate in extracurricular and enrichment activities.

However, across economic lines, many parents agree about how well they are doing raising their children. Approximately 45 percent of parents in all income brackets report that they take good care of their children. Parents "are nearly evenly divided about whether their children's successes and failures are more a reflection of how they are doing as parents (46%) or of their children's own strengths and weaknesses (42%)."[3] Parents take more responsibility for the successes and failures of younger children than for those in their teen years.

Obviously, parents are concerned for their children's education; half (53 percent) are satisfied with their level of engagement, but a substantial percentage (46 percent) wish they were doing more. About 43 percent indicate that too much parental involvement in a child's education can have negative consequences. Among parents with higher incomes, greater direct involvement in children's education is evident.

A majority of parents (62 percent) indicate that they can be overprotective, particularly from the viewpoint of the mother (68 percent compared to 54 percent for fathers). Fathers (49 percent) feel they criticize their children too much, while 39 percent of mothers feel this way. Concerning praise, 29 percent of fathers and 36 percent of mothers indicate they praise their children too much.

As mentioned earlier, 94 percent of parents want their children to be responsible—the most important character trait they cited. Finally, 70 percent of parents agree that becoming honest and ethical adults is extremely important: 65 percent want their children to be compassionate and 62 percent want them to be hardworking.

FAMILY RESILIENCE

Families do not exist in a vacuum. The Pew study specifies some of the economic and structural pressures on families. Families have to face the ups and downs of life as a collective, which include achievements, births, and milestones, as well as tragedies, deaths, and failures. The family collective must address these pressures with resilience and grit, just as individual members must.

For children, the quality of their parenting is a major factor in their attitude and disposition toward life. The resilience of families affects children's development and life perspective: "Positive parenting is a key influence on children's development,"[4] especially in difficult circumstances. How parents respond to difficulty—their attitudes and mindsets—ultimately influences the family's well-being.

Families that confront challenges and adversity and manage them successfully are considered resilient. Adapting to events certainly depends on the depth of the adversity and the strength of the family to face them.

Resilient families manage conflict and engage through positive communication and problem solving. Children in the family learn from these experiences and can see that positive analysis, action, and optimism are beneficial approaches to solve matters.

Mackay defines the aspects that make families resilient.[5] Family cohesion—strong emotional bonds between family members—is essential if families are to rise to the occasion and challenges. Positive affective involvement among family members creates connections that bind a family together in severe times.

Family belief systems, values, attitudes, convictions, biases, and assumptions prompt emotions, inform decisions, and guide choices and actions. In a sense, family culture and climate help determine actions and reactions—not too different from organizational cultures. The values and principles and the belief system determine the extent to which the family makes meaning out of hardship and forms a positive outlook on the future. The result is perseverance, persistence, optimism, hope, and confidence to overcome conditions and events—coping.

Coping is directly associated with competence and resilience and coping has two aspects: confronting a problem and limiting its impact and stress. Emotional coping is the other side that involves dealing with the psychological impact. Denying or avoiding the issue is actually an act of disengagement.

Communication, according to Mackay, is central to developing meaning in families faced with dilemmas and problems.[6] Understanding how family members perceive the outside world and their relationship to it is necessary for comprehending the issues. Without good communication, shared decision making is out of the question because clarity of expression, emotional openness, and collaboration are necessary in making decisions.

PARENTING

Parenting and family relations are complex. Parents must focus single-mindedly on the welfare of their children, sometimes at the expense of personal goals and needs. On occasion, parents must shelve their own dreams to raise children so they develop positive traits, strong character, and pertinent skills.

Resilience in children emanates from both their internal disposition and external experience. The supportive relationships with parents and others form that internal disposition, attitude, and mindset of confronting and acting, instead of withdrawing and condemning. Support from parents provides children with a sense of being able to address and master circumstances they confront with peers, teachers, and others. Quality relationships within the family help children overcome tough times.

Parenting style is often discussed and can become clichéd. Frequently, parents are faced with issues of control and warmth.[7] Authoritative parents rank high on both warmth and control and are considered optimal for children's development. Authoritarian parents, on the other hand, rank high on control and low on warmth. Permissive parents are those high on warmth and low on control. Some parents, neglectful ones, are low on both warmth and control.

Both mothers and fathers are very important: providing essential care to children and needed warmth and guidance. Children observe adults in direct action with them and learn their parents' attitudes and mind frames toward the family with its collective issues, as well as the individual challenges they confront in their own lives.

As cited earlier, fathers ranked themselves higher than mothers on criticizing their children—an indication of control. Today, however, there are more single-parent families where fathers are absent. Pruett, in his book *Fatherneed*, cites that paternal engagement is closely associated with lower incidences of disruptive behavior and acting out and with higher sociability and sense of responsibility.[8] Boys have fewer behavior problems at school and girls have a greater number of happy exchanges along with a greater capacity to try new things due, in part, to the influence of their fathers.

PARENTING OVER TIME

Older generations had a different perspective on parenting. Parenting has changed over the decades; the issue is the same, however. Parents in every era want the best for their children. The question is how to help children mature into adults who are able to adapt successfully in changing times and confront the inevitable tests that life brings.

The rise of victimhood is also related to changes in parenting. In the 1950s and 1960s, Mom would tell the kids to go out and play and be back for lunch. The 1980s brought on increased awareness and concern in the media about child safety and abductions—milk cartons displayed pictures of lost or missing children. In that time, *A Nation at Risk* was published, indicating American children were not competitive globally. Parental expectations and involvement in school increased, as well as the focus on homework and testing.

Following these approaches came the self-esteem movement: encouraging and protecting children so they feel good about themselves. The nature of play changed from what was in the 1950s and 1960s, a time when kids headed out the door to their bicycles and played in the neighborhood with friends. Parents began scheduling playdates because mothers were entering the workforce. Daycare blossomed, and playdates took place after school for children.

From this evolution came helicopter parenting, enacted by parents who were part of the baby boom generation. In the past, helicopter parenting was not prevalent. "Helicoptering" has some short-term gains—forms of safety, opportunity availability, and reciprocal outcomes. The downside is children who become parent-reliant, become sensitive to criticism and conflict, and lose a sense of self-efficacy. An overly attached mom or dad can impede maturity and independence.

Today, overparenting seems to be an issue. Teachers talk of "helicopter" parents hovering over every aspect of their child's life. Overprotective. Overseeing. Overdirecting. Overbearing. Children with helicopter parents are more likely to be medicated for depression and anxiety.[9] The child gets the idea that they do not have the ability to take care of the situation and make appropriate decisions.

Students with these hovering parents lack a belief in their own ability to reach their goals and act on their own behalf. In some cases, very good and capable students who completed and turned in assignments could not make independent decisions without specific directions from parents. Being dependent on others and failure to engage responsibly and conscientiously can be symptomatic of a larger issue like victim mentality, fear of failure, and dependency.

Children must grow and trust in themselves and act independently with a sense of self-efficiency—believing in their ability to take initiative, complete plans and work, and manage the situation as it unfolds. Self-efficiency is learned through trying, failing, and reacting to achieve the goal—resiliently responding to bounce back from falling short or failure.

In earlier decades, children were to be seen but not heard. Today's "helicopter parents" are more assertive, directing the lives of their children, which runs counter to raising a child to independence.[10]

Parents want their children to be safe, successful, and confident. They love their children, but to be overprotective, to be their children's assertive advocates, and to fight their battles for them is not healthy over the long term. Some parents act as intermediaries with teachers, officials, and others in the place of their children over grades, behavior, participation in extracurricular activities, and other issues. This takes place even with college-age students, who should be exercising their autonomy in a responsible manner. Parents, too, are concerned for their children's physical and emotional safety. Anxiety can be at the core of parental overaggressive helicoptering. They don't want them to experience mental anxiety or be fearful. They are safety-conscious, promote self-esteem, and desire academic achievement.

Hovering is not healthy: learning independence and accountability is. There is a difference between being supportive and being overbearing. Parents' own needs can get in the way. They fear being unloved or ignored unless they intervene on behalf of their children in what they consider to be a supportive way. The question is how to help children become confident and independent enough to accomplish and meet their responsibilities and goals without constant parental intervention.

Research on parenting highlights concern for children as they grow into college and beyond. In one study, college students who reported the most "helicoptering" parenting scored the lowest on a self-efficacy scale and gave the least adaptive responses to workplace scenarios. Self-efficacy is essential for mature adults. It is a belief that they have the ability to organize and take action to manage their own circumstances.

Having parents constantly intervene inhibits children from having to step up and take responsibility for their status, which is debilitating and can lead to children believing and acting as victims of circumstance. When parents take control, students can fail to develop "autonomous motivation" as opposed to the "controlled motivation" of their parents, which limits the student's ability to take charge and resolve the issues and problems they confront.[11]

The irony is that parents want their children to succeed in adulthood, but helicoptering curtails the child's ability to do well. Poor resilience, anxiety, and inadequate sense of responsibility diminish their possibility of success.

In addition, children can develop a distorted sense of entitlement. Lower demands on them to take responsibility for their issues and life lead to the belief that they are entitled to special treatment. With helicoptering, the intervention of parents or others on their behalf can give them the signal that they are special and deserving of external powers to push on their behalf.

Such poor parenting can also result in narcissism: children believing they are better than others. Thinking that they are special and requiring exceptional treatment, sometimes induced by overparenting, leads to this sense of narcissism. Relying on "parent power" to address issues of their own making raises the specter that they can rely on external power more than their own problem-solving ability. The "I have connections" syndrome is destructive and washes away children's own reliability and trustworthiness and eventually self-concept.

Parents who continually harp that their children are special and require extraordinary treatment are wrong. If their child is special, then others must not be. All children are unique—one-of-a-kind. In that sense, one child does not rise above others in terms of value, treatment, or expectation. Uniqueness is the common attribute of all human beings.

Narcissism is at work for those who adopt victim mentalities. It's the converse of "Look at me: I am great." Putting oneself down is narcissism in reverse, according to Thomas Moore. He asserts that being literally undone by failure is "negative narcissism." "The narcissist says, 'I'm a failure. I can't do anything right.' But indulgence in failure, wallowing in it rather than letting it affect the heart, is a subtle defense against the corrosive action that is essential to it and that fosters soul. By appreciating failure with imagination, we reconnected it to success. Without the connection, work falls into grand narcissistic fantasies of success and dismal feelings of failure."[12]

Ultimately, children must understand that as adults they will be responsible for their lives. Parents are not their saviors and things will not be given to them because they are "special." Helping children when they fail by discussing options and ways they can do better the next time is an important parental role. They can help them target something they want to achieve and listen to how they intend to accomplish it, while providing wise counsel. Children have to learn that success is their responsibility, not the result of parent intervention, influence, or power.

No one is happy and content all of the time. Parents cannot stop uncomfortable circumstances or negative social climates. Emotional peaks and valleys are destined to occur. "Children need to learn to manage negative emotions, and to do that, they need to experience them from time-to-time at manageable levels. The anxiety-free child is a fantasy. Anxiety is an important warning signal for potential danger. Mastering both anxiety and the thing or event that provoked it is a powerful learning experience.[13]

VICTIM MENTALITY AND PARENTS

Learning victim mentality begins in early childhood and onward; children observe adults and receive direction from them. The nature of this direction can reinforce a victim mentality or help children understand they have opportunities and control over their choices and decisions.

In early childhood, control is not within their grasp or comprehension. As they grow into their teen years, children begin to understand subtleties and abstractions better and see and feel the impact of life's events on themselves. Children grasp at this stage that they do have some control over their life and relationships and their attitudes, perceptions, and choices.

Mothers and fathers are responsible for creating an environment that is nurturing—filled with love, compassion, and joy—as children grow and develop their intellectual, emotional, and physical abilities. Growing to maturity is a process that eventually should lead to an independent, self-confident, self-controlled, and wisdom-filled life.

In some cases, parents can thwart children's ambitions and hopes through their own interactions with them. Without nurturing love, the child may demand attention and affection. Parental disparagement or constant judgment of a child's abilities and performance can circumvent any joy children experience when applying their curiosity, trying new things, or making decisions.

In many of these examples, children blame themselves for everything that happens. They adopt a sense that they cannot fall short of expectations, which leads to an attitude that enhances the chance of failure. In other words, the expectation of bad things happening can become a permanent pattern for them.

Children can learn that there is comfort in assuming a victim mentality. Parents sometimes are susceptible to sympathizing with the child in these circumstances rather than helping them examine the conditions, options, and approaches along with their responsibility and accountability.

Parents greatly influence children's development and attitudes.

> Depending on their own sense of victimhood, parents can either create a supportive, trustful environment for their children, or do exactly the opposite and perpetuate a bad situation. Thus they create a generational problem of victimhood, in which secondary gain gets the upper hand. For children growing up in these family situations, suffering is a way of soliciting attention and forestalling parental criticism and indifference. It makes for a paradoxical relational style in which life seems to improve when it is going badly. The parents become kinder when the child feels bad. Presenting a suffering exterior gives the child respite from an otherwise hostile and neglectful family environment. Parenthood comes with certain obligations. We can't ignore the basic needs and rights of our children. We expect adults to take a stand against abuse and create a different developmental cycle.[14]

Even with authoritative parents, experiencing adolescence and growing into early adulthood is not without incident or crises. Peers place pressure to conform in a variety of areas. Trying to find a balance between honoring parental goals and creating a self-identity is not always fluid and easy.

For children who have lost a parent, it is more difficult to create a self without an example or assistance. Eleanor Roosevelt, for example, had to define herself, almost out of necessity, because she had been orphaned and parental guidance was lacking. Some of these children feel that they have to "go it alone"; unlike those with victim mentality, they become very self-reliant, which has its own possible complications.

Harris indicates:

> The ability to embrace the entirety of one's fate may take a variety of different forms. For some, the acceptance of who one is comes after a period of struggle. These individuals reclaim a destiny they once felt was lost. For others, there is an ongoing tension between personal control and fate. Still others seem to be survivor proud, possessing a sense of personal accomplishment at having survived tragedy.[15]

In a broader sense, parents want their children to be able to self-actualize and lead a fulfilling life. That includes growing and understanding themselves and living with character and compassion. Love is an essential part of life—that which comes from an individual's heart. But there is also another type of love, "agape," which concerns charity and an act of will to live with compassion and commitment to others.[16] Seeing the wonder of the world and humanity affects how individuals react toward others. Good will is a character trait and a form of unconditional love with no expectation of reciprocation.

SO WHAT CAN PARENTS DO?

Parents' jobs are not to make excuses for their kids, cloak them in smothering love, or succumb to every whiny plea for something. In some families, children are directing traffic and controlling their parents. Who would have guessed that four- and five-year-olds would be bargaining with their adult parent and winning! Certainly, this impairs the climate for children's positive development and character growth and raises dilemmas for them in the future.

A first step is to create a family culture of accountability. This doesn't have to sound or be harsh because ultimately in life, it cannot be avoided. Parents need to take control—actually, children really want that, too. Children need opportunities to try difficult things and solve problems. They need to know that they have choices and that those choices are based on values and principles—honesty, hard work, and responsibility—and come with consequences. Parents should teach them the skills and approaches to solve problems. They must be sure not to respond to their children's blaming and self-victimization—instead, they should recognize the situation and reassure them they can work themselves out of it.

Some children want a reprieve from any rules—they feel that the rules shouldn't apply to them. In some cases, teens feel that parents are the reason for their problems. In their minds, parent regulations, expectations, and direction created their circumstances: not their own actions or decisions. "It's not my fault, if you did/didn't . . ." or "My other friend's parents let them . . ." These teens are applying a "thinking error" and getting the wrong answer to life situations. Thinking errors include: justification, dishonesty, excuses, and accusing.[17]

Parents are collaborators—knowing or unknowing—when they allow their children to engage in the victim-thinking error. Accepting their excuses is distracting them from their accountability for the issue at hand. Parents can respond by saying: "Making excuses is not going to solve the problem of you having to mow the lawn, and I expect you to do it" or "Blaming your teacher is not going to solve your problem of getting your homework done."[18] In these two cases, the parent is pointing out that excuses and blaming are thinking errors in solving the problem at hand. In some cases, parents can express, "Just your luck, you have parents who are not sheep and have expectations for you. We do not care how other parents raise their kids. Just as we want you to be an independent thinker, we, as parents, don't really care or go along with the pack of other parents."

Another important concept is helping children understand what is and what is not within their control. For example, graduation requirements in math are beyond an individual's control, but the selection of courses and the work necessary to pass them are not. It is very important that children hear from parents and others the phrase, "I believe in you and I will stand by you." Resilient children, according to research, need an adult available to provide support by promoting connection and helping them overcome feelings of isolation.

Brooks and Goldstein sum up ways parents can change their children's negative perspectives. The guideposts embedded in the mindset of parents who foster resilience in their youngsters include:

- being empathic
- communicating effectively and listening actively
- changing "negative scripts"
- loving their children in ways that help them to feel appreciated
- accepting children for who they are and helping them to set realistic expectations and goals
- helping children experience success by identifying and reinforcing their "islands of competence"
- helping children recognize that mistakes are experiences from which to learn
- developing responsibility, compassion, and a social conscience by providing children with opportunities to contribute
- teaching children to solve problems and make decisions

- disciplining in a way that promotes self-discipline and self-worth[19]

POINTS TO REMEMBER

- Over 90 percent of parents indicate that being responsible is the most important trait they want their children to develop.
- The quality of parenting is a key influence in children's development.
- Family cohesion—strong emotional bonds—is essential if families are to rise to the occasion in difficult times. Family culture and climate determine behavior.
- Parental support provides children with a sense of being able to confront and master circumstances.
- Overprotecting, overseeing, overdirecting, or overparenting can have negative consequences for children in developing independence and a sense of self-efficacy.
- Children must understand that ultimately they are responsible for their lives. Success is their responsibility, not the result of others' influence, intervention, or power.
- Parents must be aware that children can learn from them that there is comfort in adopting a victim mentality by soliciting sympathy and attention and forestalling criticism.
- Parents must help their children examine situations and options and their responsibilities and accountability.
- Parents must establish a family culture of accountability and help children understand what is and what is not under their individual control.
- Parents should not allow their children to use "thinking errors" to avert responsibility.

NOTES

1. James O'Toole, *Creating the Good Life* (New York: Rodale, 2005), 49.
2. Pew Research Center, "Parenting in America," December 17, 2015, http://www.pewsocialtrends.org/2015/12/17/1-the-american-family-today/.
3. Ibid.
4. Ross Mackay, "Family Resilience and Good Child Outcomes: An Overview of the Research Literature," *Social Policy Journal of New Zealand* 20 (June 2003): 98.
5. Ibid., 102–6.
6. Ibid., 105–6.
7. Ibid., 108.
8. Kyle D. Pruett, *Fatherneed* (New York: Broadway Books, 2000), 52.
9. Julie Lythcott-Haims, *How to Raise an Adult: Break Free of the Overparenting Trap and Prepare Your Kid for Success* (New York: Henry Holt and Company, 2015), Kindle edition, loc. 1683.
10. Jill C. Bradley-Geist and Julie B. Olson-Buchanan, "Helicopter Parents: An Examination of the Correlates of Over-parenting College Students," *Education and Training* 56, no. 4 (2014): 314 28.

11. Richard Koestner, Nancy Otis, Theodore A. Powers, Luc Pelletier, and Hugo Gagnon, "Autonomous Motivation, Controlled Motivation, and Goal Progress," *Journal of Personality* 76, no. 5 (October 2008): 1201–30.

12. Thomas Moore, *Care of the Soul* (New York: HarperPerennial, 1992), 197.

13. Kyle D. Pruett, *Me, Myself and I* (New York: Gotthard Press, 1999), 81.

14. Manfred F. R. Kets de Vries, "Are You a Victim of the Victim Syndrome?" faculty and research working paper, INSEAD, 2012, https://sites.insead.edu/facultyresearch/research/doc.cfm?did=50114.

15. Maxine Harris, *The Loss That Is Forever* (New York: Penguin, 1996), Kindle edition, 291.

16. Fred Kofman, *Conscious Business: How to Build Value through Values* (Boulder, CO: Sounds True, 2006), 284.

17. James Lehman, "I'm a Victim, so the Rules Don't Apply to Me," Empowering Parents, August 2, 2012, https://www.empoweringparents.com/article/im-a-victim-so-the-rules-dont-apply-to-me-how-to-stop-victim-thinking-in-kids/.

18. Ibid.

19. Robert Brooks and Sam Goldstein, *Resilient Children: Fostering Strength, Hope and Optimism in Your Child* (New York: McGraw-Hill Education, 2001), Kindle edition, loc. 227.

Chapter Nine

Flourish or Languish

"To live is the rarest thing in the world. Most people exist, that is all." —Oscar Wilde

Success does produce happiness. Scoring the winning basket, touchdown, or goal produces a rush of euphoria. Those accomplishments, for some, can become the center focus and achievement of their lives. The pinnacle moment! Some live the rest of their lives just reliving that event. Notoriety at a young age can color children's viewpoints that success should come easy. These individuals can become "one-hit wonders" or people who achieved their peak and recognition at a very young age and never moved ahead to other challenges.

Some parents and others tell their kids the depressing notion that high school "was the best years of your life." This insinuates that the remaining sixty to seventy years are all "downhill." Not a very promising perspective. In such cases, happiness becomes short-lived and doesn't translate into true meaning or long-term significance.

Life, however, is not served in equal portion sizes. There are going to be times of abundance, as well as periods of scarcity. For the "one-hit wonders," the idea that things may not always come easy, or that other people might develop physically or intellectually and outperform them, is not on their radar.

Other children struggle in high school but later become renowned for their accomplishments in their fields. Achieving positive results after struggle and exhaustive effort can result in continued success and a sense of perspective. The first successful result can be more rewarding and reinforce the concept that confronting difficult issues and succeeding, even with initial frustration, can be extremely rewarding and satisfying. The concept that if it happened once it can certainly happen again can generate more determination and hard work.

Success and its pathways may entail the exploration of many favorable and promising things. Even if the activities end in lack of success, that does not mean that happiness and a good life cannot be found. The journey itself may be joyful and enlightening—learning new things and gaining wisdom and greater self-understanding.

Joy exists in the journey with the support of others. The love expressed in those relationships and moments is powerful: it's a time when strong character and moral imperatives take precedence over the materialistic and mundane. A good life is about loving relationships and passionate purpose.

A basic question in the pursuit is: What is there to live for? For those trapped in a victim mentality with their self-defeating assumptions, the answers to that question are bleak.[1] Their attitudes are reflective of their assumptions: "I am dumb," "If I try, it will not make a difference," "You can't trust those people," and "Why try when the deck is stacked?" People cannot be fulfilled in absentia if they are above the fray and do not participate.

The initiative to begin the pursuit is destroyed and negates any positive personal or social consequences that can result. In addition, any talent the individual has becomes buried or undeveloped. Being cradled in fear or covered in the blanket of arrogance is not benign behavior for anyone. Not owning their actions implies no responsibility and a rejection of the control they have over their choices and behavior.

Children must grow to realize that their lives can and will change. There are things beyond high school and its social interactions to live for. Do they have any creative calling or work they wish to investigate or complete? Is there a relationship waiting for them that they want to experience? Are there issues that stimulate commitment and creativity? Victim mentality does not lead to emotional or physical wellness but results in intellectual and spiritual emptiness.

HAPPINESS AND MEANING

The Centers for Disease Control in a survey of Americans found that four of ten have not found life satisfying.[2] They do not have a clear sense of purpose that increases satisfaction with life, which also affects their physical and mental health. "People with high levels of positive emotions, and those who are functioning well psychologically and socially are described by some as having complete mental health or 'flourishing.'"[3]

Well-being includes the presence of positive emotions and moods—contentment and happiness. There is a sense of fulfillment and satisfaction with life—a sense that they have functioned positively in pursuing their calling. A calling requires accepting and following through on responsibilities, and it provides reasons to live fully by confronting and responding to challenges with resilience. Love is a powerful force and motivator, as well as a core of happiness and acceptance.

Happiness is based on the drive to satisfy a desire, for example to have a comfortable, warm, and safe home. When satisfied, this brings a feeling of happiness. So does a new car or going on a relaxing vacation. In a sense in seeking happiness, individuals are "takers" satisfying their individual desires.

Meaning, on the other hand, transcends self and focuses on contributing to others or to important causes. Meaning has a clearly defined purpose or mission. Self-interest is not the motivation. Serving others, a principle, or a cause is the focus. In finding meaning, there is more to life than self-focused happiness, and it may require self-sacrifice and conflict and even the possibility of suffering.

Happiness and meaningfulness are linked by such factors as feeling connected to others, feeling productive, and not being bored or alone.[4] The two concepts, however, are distinct. Happiness is generally focused on feeling good in the present. Meaningfulness, however, integrates the past, present, and future and, at times, may involve feeling bad due to past misfortunes in pursuing commitment to others, ideals, and causes.

In pursuing meaningful causes, individuals may sacrifice short-term desires and comfort. Worthy goals sometimes require inconveniences and the reduction of comforts or pleasures. In other words, difficult undertakings can result in stress, worry, anxiety, and conflict. Thoughtful consideration of past and future circumstances is necessary when looking beyond self-interest.

Being involved with serious causes rests on a commitment to giving something back to society or others or to making progress on important objectives or movements. Doing things of meaning is actually an expression of "self" because they define what the individual's commitments and principles are: what they stand for positively and to what purpose they dedicate their time, knowledge, and skills.

Meaningfulness can be both emotional and cognitive, requiring critical and creative thinking and passion and fervor. Individuals are, by and large, self-regulating in analyzing circumstances, actions, and outcomes and committing their talent and effort to them.

On another front, people can live very happy but relatively meaningless lives. Individuals can be totally carefree without stress or anxiety, without any thought of the past or the future or the bigger picture. Things go well, needs and desires are fulfilled, and no uncomfortable complications get in the way. In some respects, life can center on self-absorbing activities and shallow relationships and ventures—recreation, dinner, entertainment, and others.

A meaningful life is reflective of the person's character and priorities: it has a cultural base or imperative geared to future goal realization or attainment. Immediate gratification is not in the cards. A greater good is the focus. Meaning can be a source of stability in the continuous fluctuation of life. A sense of efficacy—that one can make a difference—is apparent in finding meaning and addressing the moral imperative to be a good person and lead a good life.

FLOURISHING VS. LANGUISHING

While many assume that happiness is the ultimate goal in life, it is conceivable to be happy but not to flourish. People can succeed and not lead a good or worthwhile life. Physical health is certainly a part of a good life, but mental and social well-being are also necessary.

Individuals who are mentally healthy have "positive levels of feelings and psychosocial functioning . . . and live . . . within an optimal range of human functioning, one that connotes goodness, generativity, growth, and resilience."[5] A positive emotion about life is evident—emotional well-being, psychological well-being, and social well-being. People with these qualities have excellent emotional health and place fewer restrictions on themselves when investing in their interests and life.

Fewer than 25 percent of people between the ages of twenty-five and seventy-four state that they fit the criteria for flourishing: having a positive emotion toward life and functioning well socially and psychologically. An individual who is "devoid of positive emotion toward life, is not functioning well psychologically or socially and has not been depressed during the past year" is languishing.[6] Victim mentality fits the bill for languishing.

Languishers do not necessarily live a bad life, and they are not clinically depressed. They have a feeling of hollowness and emptiness. It is the absence of positive mental health but not a state of mental illness. As indicated, people in this state may have a good job, meet their physical needs, and attain their desires. But nonetheless, weariness about life surrounds them and they are listless in its pursuit. Many feel a bit lost and without purpose—adrift.

Children can feel this, too. They can languish. Socioeconomic status is not a factor. This feeling can occur among all children across all socioeconomic and ethnic groups. A documentary on PBS's *Frontline*, "The Lost Children of Rockdale County," which won a Peabody Award for journalism, highlights the lives of teenagers in Rockdale County, Georgia. The story is focused on an outbreak of syphilis in this community, where parents are economically successful, complete with nice houses and neighborhoods and good schools.

This documentary, while initially focused on the unexpected syphilis outbreak among the teenagers, highlights the increasing alienation and loneliness of students who were unanchored and adrift despite their social and economic status and demonstrated an emptiness of purpose. They had a sense that they were not needed by or engaged to adults, to tasks, or to anything other than the raw and relentless pursuit of pleasure. Substance was absent and pleasures were hollow and destructive. Eventually, the hollowness fractures self-image and relationships with others, including parents.

Teenagers and adults can live in quiet despair because of the absence of purpose and consequence. Goals and ambition are nonexistent, as are principles and values.

The lack of positive purpose leads to dysfunctional behavior as in the Rockdale example. Enthusiasm for life is lacking even when physical comforts and needs are met.

Flourishing is much like achieving self-actualization. Individuals desire personal growth and apply their autonomy to solve issues that contribute to the greater good. A positive affect about life and the ability to effect change and resolve issues are prevalent. Personal growth, not stagnation, is a marker of individuals who find direction and significance in life. They are engaged and not sitting languishing on the sidelines.

People who flourish in life are generally optimists while those with a victim mentality see life's choices through a negative and pessimistic lens. Optimism is linked to happiness, achievement, and perseverance. Perseverance is important because life has challenges and dead ends. People who flourish are not without difficult and frustrating times or severe losses. In fact, research demonstrates that if children can learn to be less pessimistic and solve problems, they can become more resilient.[7]

Rising to challenges at home or work requires grit: working through tough times and suffering can instill a sense of self-efficacy. In many cases, these individuals have to assert themselves and be dependable, open-minded, and self-confident in confronting tribulations. A positive can-do spirit is embraced and evident.

The lesson is: confronting and working through issues affects self-perception and makes individuals more self-assured and self-reliant. Gaining a sense of self-understanding about being vulnerable, along with an appreciation of the assistance of others, helps discriminate between minor problems or issues and what is really important.

In everyone's life, there are decisive turning points: times when people find things out about themselves that are important for them to hear. Sometimes they are negative or sometimes positive and reinforcing perspectives. Even if feedback is upsetting, these circumstances help individuals learn what is important in relationships and in life. Self-realization and emotion are painted in clear lines so they can sustain positive or change negative attitudes and behavior.

The individual's mentors or polestars, who are a part of these turning-point circumstances, care for the person and give them difficult feedback because they want them to apply their unrealized potential and succeed.

The upshot of a good life—a flourishing life—is a sense of well-being. The elements of well-being are not going to be found in a stifling passive-aggressive life. In fact, victim mentality is the utter opposite of the mindset necessary to find well-being.

Positive emotion coupled with engagement is the foundation for life satisfaction. Being engaged in a task or challenge involves serving or belonging to something larger then self. Positive relationships create joy—through working with other people on purposeful work.

Finally, being engaged significantly in experiences that are intensely focused and are rewarding regardless of outcome is called flow. The activity is totally absorbing in itself and brings a sense of satisfaction, whether it be creative or artistic or working with others on matters of importance. It is enjoyed and meaningful.

People who flourish find a sense of virtue and wisdom that addresses issues of conduct and meaning in life. Knowledge is certainly a component of wisdom, but that alone is not a sufficient definition. Wisdom involves conceptualization of principles and virtues that are lived and acted on with character. Ethical understanding involves comprehending that at times two positive principles can clash, creating ethical dilemmas—for example, right versus right, such as the conflict between privacy or security.

Wisdom and humility are connected. Humility has a component of freedom to it. Contrary to egotism, humble individuals are free from having the need to prove their superiority. Actually, "humility is the awareness that there is a lot you don't know and that a lot of what you think you know is distorted or wrong."[8]

Humility leads to wisdom in the sense that it has a moral quality to it: knowing what one doesn't know and how to handle the ignorance and uncertainty. Wise people overcome their biases and arrogance. Acting with character and integrity is a part of wisdom: knowing how to decide and act when knowledge is lacking.

Leading a good life, however, is not just about the "self." Today, the word "I" projects narcissism: victim mentality is all about "I." There are other issues, however, that go beyond "I."

Being self-centered is a way to be cut off from others on two fronts. First, other individuals will not be attracted to certain people who are engrossed in their own narrow interests and issues. Secondly, other people want friends or colleagues who make commitments beyond themselves and are positive contributors.

Acting responsibly and taking responsibility are necessary for a sense of community and the common good. Character and virtue do matter and go beyond self-interest. Self-control is essential in overcoming victim mentality.

Brooks states, "Character is built in the course of your inner confrontation. Character is a set of dispositions, desires, and habits that are slowly engraved during the struggle against your own weakness. You become more disciplined, considerate, and loving through small acts of self-control, sharing, service, friendship, and refined enjoyment."[9]

People do not live pristine lives free of failure, loss, or weakness. Sometimes it is difficult for individuals to parse all of the subtleties that create larger, tangible consequences. Life is complex with energy systems of emotion, attitudes, or intentions at work.

The relatively small decision of one individual withdrawing into a victim mentality can have a butterfly effect. Their relatively minor or small choice can create a wave of lifetime regret and possibly stop a greater good because of one individual's resistance to being response-able. Then the loss is not just one person's failure but a greater one—the loss of purpose and meaning that can affect family and the greater good.

One possible result of victim mentality that relates to languishing is stagnation, which can occur in children as they grow and move to greater independence. They can experience disconnection from others and a larger social scene.

The result of stagnation is a lack of connection to others and a feeling of loneliness. As people age, living in isolation with no sense of commitment or contribution to caring for others or making their world a better place is debilitating. People need to be needed.

POINTS TO REMEMBER

- Failure can lead to success and encourage and develop determination and commitment to hard work.
- In pursuing meaningful causes, individuals may sacrifice short-term desires and comfort. Meaning concerns what individuals stand for and to what purpose they dedicate their time, knowledge, and skills. A sense of efficacy results.
- People can live happily; however, lives focused on the carefree, the stress-free, and the present can be meaningless.
- Flourishing involves emotional well-being, psychological well-being, and social well-being. It is conceivable for people to be happy and yet not flourish.

- Languishing is being devoid of positive emotion toward life and not functioning well psychologically or socially. Individuals feel hollow and empty; however, it is not a state of mental illness or depression.
- Teenagers can feel adrift, empty of purpose, not connected to adults, and devoid of purpose. Hollowness results.
- Flourishing is much like self-actualization: self-growth and applying autonomy to issues that contribute to the common good. Personal growth, not stagnation, is the marker.
- Wisdom entails the convergence of virtue and process that produces excellence personally and for the common good.
- Victim mentality is diametrically opposed to the qualities required to flourish in life.

NOTES

1. Robert Brooks and Sam Goldstein, *The Power of Resilience: Achieving Balance, Confidence, and Personal Strength in Your Life* (New York: McGraw-Hill Education, 2004), Kindle edition, loc. 3824.
2. Centers for Disease Control and Prevention, "Health-Related Quality of Life: Well-Being Concepts," last modified May 31, 2016, https://www.cdc.gov/hrqol/wellbeing.htm.
3. Ibid.
4. Roy F. Baumeister, Kathleen D. Vohs, Jennifer L. Aaker, and Emily N. Garbinsky, "Some Key Differences between a Happy Life and a Meaningful Life," *The Journal of Positive Psychology* 8, no. 6 (August 30, 2013): 505–16.
5. Corey L. M. Keyes and Jonathan Haidt, eds., *Flourishing: Positive Psychology and the Life Well-Lived* (Washington, DC: American Psychological Association, 2002), Kindle edition, loc. 6061–72.
6. Ibid., loc. 6072.
7. Ibid., loc. 1636.
8. David Brooks, *The Road to Character* (New York: Random House, 2015), Kindle edition, 266.
9. Ibid., 263.

Chapter Ten

Managing Life

"Without experiencing the rougher spots of life, our kids become exquisite, like orchids, yet are incapable, sometimes terribly incapable, of thriving in the real world on their own." —Julie Lythcott-Haims

"As far as the laws of mathematics refer to reality, they are not certain, and as far as they are certain, they do not refer to reality." —Albert Einstein

Just after the 2016 presidential election, a sixteen-year-old girl who was a junior in high school visited her grandparents in Connecticut. She was beginning to think about colleges and the application process. As part of the discussion, her grandfather encouraged her to apply to a number of colleges, including the possibility of those in the Ivy League.

He suggested that they drive to Yale and take a tour of the college. So the next day, off they went to New Haven. At the visitor center, they listened to a student-led discussion about Yale, along with a video of what the school had to offer.

As part of the presentation, a student led a tour of the entire campus, along with an interesting history of the school's beginning and historical contributions. Both of the girl's grandparents were college educated, and the grandfather earned a bachelor's and advanced degrees during the Vietnam War era.

The tour eventually came to the beautiful library. As the student guide explained the history surrounding the facility, the grandfather noticed writings in chalk on the pavement in the courtyard in front of the library. One comment written in huge multicolored letters proclaimed, "You Are Loved."

Strange, he thought, how different times are. When he was in college, there were high-velocity, passionate, and often violent demonstrations against the Vietnam War. Students took an independent stand against par-

ents and others and protested. Now, he couldn't believe that students needed an affirmation that they are "loved." From that controversial war-era perspective complete with concern for the military draft, campus violence, and political conflict, today's students, because of a surprise election result, need to be told that they are "loved"?

Today there are other examples of the apparent "orchid-like" delicateness of the upcoming generation. Some indicate it is the result of coddling, overparenting, and protecting children against difficulty and challenges. As indicated earlier, helicopter parents can restrict the growth of their children to become resilient and response-able. Facing unexpected and undesired outcomes or situations seems to have thrown some young adults and others into a frenzy.

On college campuses today, students raise concerns of "micro-aggressions" if instructors present issues, class content, or readings that they feel are uncomfortable or disconcerting. Student safety has expanded to being protected from being offended over the academic content, presentations, and debate. Fear of offending students and giving "trigger" warnings are examples of orchid-like behavior. Universities have historically been havens of free speech, ideas, and debate. Some professors feel caught between the ideal of free speech and crippling self-censorship.[1]

Other individuals and those from generations past had to face far more difficult, and sometimes life-threatening, situations beyond the outcome of an election or classroom content. In a piece in the *New York Times*, Arthur Brook discusses the hazards of a "victimhood culture" where "activists interpret ordinary interactions as 'micro-aggressions' and set up 'safe spaces' to protect students from certain forms of speech."[2] A victimhood culture destroys a society of give-and-take dialogue and turns it into good versus evil battles. Actually, he states that such a culture creates victim entitlement that can result in a sense of selfishness: individuals feel more entitled because of their perceived unfair treatment.

The rise of victim culture is, in part, due to societal conditions and media, which enable the ability to complain and demand help from others. Instantaneous and rapid-fire social media sites explode with immediate reactions. Clarity and thoughtful analysis fall victim to gut responses as the media's priority is getting the so-called story out first. Responsibility for any error, incorrect commentary, speculation, or partisan pabulum is nowhere to be found. Supreme Court Justice Thomas states, "In the long run, a society that abandons personal responsibility will lose its moral sense."[3]

Assuming victimhood is geared to gathering sympathy and diverting responsibility or, at times, limiting speech. Those who take the victim route curtail their individual ability to act and respond by receding into their shell of victimization. Speech is then limited to what cannot be construed in any manner as offensive, controversial, or hurtful. In a curious way, that position itself can be victimizing: not treating individuals as mature adults.

Being offended and challenged is a part of life. Growing to maturity is learning how to deal with it without falling into self-victimhood and exaggerating circumstances and events. Victim mentality is not creative. Blaming is not a strategy. "Turtle-ing" is not a plan or a solution. In reality, they create a loss of credibility and integrity that curtails effectiveness and respect. Life goes on whether those with victim mentality like it or not.

ORCHIDS OR DANDELIONS?

Raising children is not easy, but neither is life. Parents know that their child is bound to face some difficult times and that to survive and thrive adaptability and toughness are necessary. The issue is how parents can raise children to be able to withstand and respond to the unpredictability of life.

Researchers identified children who can deal successfully with the pressure of circumstances and those who have difficulty and trauma. Ellis and Boyce use a floral metaphor to categorize children into two types: the orchid child and the dandelion child.[4]

Dandelion children are resilient and have the capacity to survive and even thrive in the various contexts and environments they experience. Orchid children are highly sensitive to their environment and to the quality and nature of parenting and support. They wither if they are neglected, but on the other hand, they may flourish in conditions they perceive to be stress-free and safe. Pressures and tough situations can debilitate the orchids.

The problem is that life is not or ever will be stress-free. The issue is how all parents can effectively help their children through tough times and problems so they become resilient. Keeping a positive perspective can help children discover options in difficult conditions. These moments provide the opportunity to teach children how to approach and respond to situations initially and in the aftermath.

Children need verbal and nonverbal support when facing pressure and thorny and complex conditions. Being open to new approaches helps them learn, problem solve, and see alternatives, along with identifying their assets and deficits.

Society is not an environmentally controlled greenhouse free of conflict, demands, or physical and psychological stress. Sensitive children, whether genetically disposed or not, need to discover the means to address the pressure and circumstance and apply their skills and aptitude effectively. Cohesive and adaptive families and parents can help them become independent. Continued support from family and others enables children to confront and adapt to life's traumas as active "players," not hapless victims.

Chapter 10
CHAOTIC SYSTEMS

The saying "the best laid plans of mice and men . . ." from Robert Burns's 1786 poem pretty well expresses how life plays out. What is expected as normal events of life sometimes never occur, and if they do, they may arise through unexpected events or happenings. Life's serendipity can result in both fortune and misfortune.

The fact of the matter is that society is a chaotic system in which small changes and differences can create divergent and sometimes major unexpected outcomes. Data, algorithms, or philosophical projections cannot always predict life. It doesn't always follow a linear path, but it is complex and filled with emotion, relationships, and sometimes seemingly small factors that can effect major changes. Human beings are complicated and evolving beings who are not always easy to figure out or predict.

When the unexpected or unpredictable happens, children and adults can't just fall onto the floor in a heap or expect someone to protect them. Everyone is born with the power to respond and work to change things.

As in chaos theory, the idea that one small change can alter outcomes also applies to individuals. In chaos theory, the butterfly effect is caused by small changes that bring about dramatic changes. The stock market, society, and weather are examples of nonlinear systems that are not always predictable. Life, too, is nonlinear and is not always predictable: sometimes change, chance meetings, or unexpected events dramatically alter people's lives.

History is illustrative—both positively and negatively—of the power of individuals. People, individually or collectively, have imagination, ingenuity, intelligence, and free will with which to respond to what life brings. An internal locus of control—the ability to look inside themselves and see that they are response–able—is a very important perspective required to adapt and succeed. An individual with an external locus of control believes that success, failure, or circumstances are the result of outside factors beyond control—fate, luck, bias, injustice, or individuals like teachers, bosses, politicians, or the "system."

An internal locus of control enables individuals to develop ideas, plans, and strategies to effect change and circumstances and react to butterfly effects. They can act—not become passive and defenseless victims. Self-efficacy is believing that through goal-directed action, an individual's actions can impact challenging or stressful circumstances.

Survivors think differently from those with a victim mentality: they simply do not place obstacles in the way of their own efficacy nor do they muddle with excuses. They understand that pressing issues may take time and stamina. Change does not happen overnight.

Survivors self-reflect and try to determine how they arrived at the situation they face, and whether they could have done more to influence or avert it. They are positive and try to find ways to make good things happen. An optimistic and constructive perspective is evident, not a "woe is me" attitude: they understand that not everything works out as desired or planned.

Survivors accept responsibility, learn from mistakes, and find ways to improve, in addition to being able to take constructive criticism and advice. Finally, survivors do not malign others but act with forgiveness to those who may have stood in their way or harmed them. They seek solutions and do not languish in the cloud of self-inflicted victimhood.

SELF-MANAGEMENT

Self-managing life takes adaptability and determination. The external locus of control perspective or the pursuit of sympathy or the avoidance of responsibility destines individuals to suffocate from the impotence to consciously influence outcomes. Self-management and self-efficacy are surrendered, along with any real prospect of success.

Everyone, including children at certain ages, should look in the mirror and ask whether they are spending their time wisely and how they have addressed and confronted issues and pressure. "Knowing thyself" requires periodically self-assessing perspectives, attitudes, and behavior. This can be revealing.

Self-assessment and reflection are necessary for everyone in all positions and dispositions in life. Kaplan recommends several questions individuals should ask themselves:[5]

- How often do I examine my goals and key priorities to achieve them?
- Does the way I spend my time match my priorities?
- How do I behave under pressure?
- Am I attuned to changes in my family, school, and social group that require a shift in my behavior?
- Does my behavior reflect who I am as a person?
- Looking back, how could I have acted differently in light of the circumstances in order to get a better result?
- Do I assert myself appropriately?
- How do I react when people give me feedback?
- Do others see me as optimistic or pessimistic?
- How do my emotions affect others—teachers, parents, friends, and others?
- Do people see me as authentic?
- What signals am I sending to parents, friends, teachers, and others? Do they undermine my relationships?

Asking these questions helps students begin a process of self-reflection that has continued relevance throughout each stage of life and relates to emotional intelligence.

Goldman et al. cite four important components of emotional intelligence in responding to events.[6]

First, self-awareness entails being able to "read" one's own emotions. People then know their strengths and weaknesses and build self-confidence. These individuals realize and understand how they are affecting others.

Second, self-management is vitally important. The ability to control emotions and behave honorably and with integrity is critical in the process of adapting to situations and dealing with conflict.

Third, social awareness and empathy, as well as intuition, can guide people in sensing other's emotions and reading the tenor of situations and relationships. Learning to understand the impact of words and actions on others helps to determine the reaction to people and events.

Finally, managing relationships by communicating clearly and appropriately can disarm conflict and build bonds between people. Individuals who cut themselves off from others will not be able to prosper in social situations at school, home, or work.

Parents and others can help children examine their behavior and status by asking several questions.[7]

- What kind of person do I want to be and what do I have to do to get there?
- Who am I now? What are my strengths and weaknesses?
- How do I get from here to there? What's the plan, who can assist me, and what experiences will help?
- How do I make change stick? In reviewing past situations, was my behavior appropriate? What and how could it have changed?
- Who can help me? What individuals or groups? Who will listen actively to help?

These questions are applicable to individuals of all ages and development. Individuals with a victim mentality have to get out of their bubble and begin to self-manage themselves and their lives. Self-management—taking control and direction of life—is absolutely essential for maturity and independence in a changing and sometimes chaotic environment.

THE POWER OF PURPOSE

Part of finding purpose is answering the philosophical question—"Why am I here?" Children wrestle with this question as they work their way through school. High schoolers begin to try to figure out where they fit in a variety of areas: family, relationships, socially, career, mission, and their own individual satisfaction with life.

Finding a calling in life is not easy. It doesn't just pop out of a textbook or a lesson. "Purpose clarifies our calling. It gives meaning to our work. We know why we get up in the morning."[8] Calling is discovered by taking advantage of opportunities, trying new things, applying talents, meeting new people, getting advice from others, and, importantly, acting without fear of failure.

An education and being exposed to ideas, subject matter content, research, philosophy, and creative arts can light the candle of purpose. Purpose does not always come through an "aha" moment; sometimes it is given birth slowly through traversing the peaks and valleys of life.

In many cases, purpose comes in the form of small, and sometimes seemingly inconsequential, events or experiences. But nonetheless, purpose becomes clear if individuals think and feel and react: victories as well as defeats and a variety of experiences can be the spark that jolts them into realization. Struggles and chaos can present opportunities where talent, values, principles, and mission call to them.

Within all people is a small voice of creativity that moves them in finding and pursuing aspirations. That is why children should listen to what calls them and not always pay attention to the chatter of society and peer groups or the expectations of others.

All individuals have something to live for: purpose provides meaning and meaning provides the satisfaction and energy to contribute to something greater than themselves. What they live for defines the relevance of their lives far more than simply acquiring sustenance and material goods. Actually, "it is the opportunity to learn, grow in responsibilities, contribute to others and be recognized for achievements" that provides meaning and happiness.[9]

A sense of purpose drives each of these and determines how individuals spend their time and apply their skills, talent, and energy. "If you are not guided by a clear sense of purpose, you're likely to fritter away your time and energy on obtaining the most tangible, short-term signs of achievement, not what's really important to you."[10] One's work and commitment to act, social issues, spiritual issues, or relationships provide the meaning people strive for in pursuing a life of goodness.

Striving toward meaningful goals in life is not the recipe for immediate gratification. Actually, immediate gratification can deflect time and resources to irrelevant or meaningless issues and endeavors. Everyone has choices that they make that will either enhance meaning or squander time, energy, and resources on side trips.

Chapter 10
STRATEGIES FOR HELPING STUDENTS

Growing into adulthood is challenging, and living an adult life of meaning and purpose isn't any easier. Helping children discover who they are and why they are here as unique, one-of-a-kind human beings is a challenge. Helping children to eventually find their purpose is much more complex and abstract.

Teachers have become so focused on material outcomes and data that there is the fear that tangible metrics will cause schools to lose the ability to spur thought about abstract notions like purpose and meaning. Philosophy, unfortunately, is not even discussed as a subject in secondary schools. While metrics can be helpful, it is ideas, values, and principles that move history and individual lives.

Teachers, parents, and others can do some things to help children develop into response-able people who have a mission in life to which they are committed. Thinking is powerful—and as students mature, it should become more complex, incorporating abstract, concrete, and practical reasoning.

At certain ages, it is appropriate to have conversations with students about life and purpose. After all, when they are finished with formal education, they will be applying those thoughts and knowledge every day for the rest of their lives. They surely think about their aspirations as they traverse their high school years and gain greater autonomy. They must realize that a sense of purpose develops over time and does not happen by a specific calendar date. For some it becomes clear early; for others it may take decades.

School and family cultures are powerful, as they are in organizations and corporations. Children react to structures and cultures. If the culture is respectful toward each individual, then children will feel free to express themselves, their ideas, and their concerns. Problems and fears will also be raised because of the sense of safety and support. The same is true of classrooms and the care teachers demonstrate.

One lesson that is imperative is to teach children about integrity. From early years through high school and beyond, learning that one does not compromise principles and values is essential to being perceived by others as a person of integrity. If children see adults say one thing and then act in opposite ways, they are learning the wrong lesson.

Pressure from social groups is difficult and can confound situations and pressure individuals to do what is popular or easy, rather than what is right. Standing alone on principle is not always easy or well received, and taking any rebuke or challenge takes courage. People pulled into a victim mentality and falling into a passive shell lose any sense of integrity.

Resilient individuals act with a sense of self-esteem. They who know themselves and feel good about it have a sense of humility. They view others with a sense of regard and realize that they can learn from them. Arrogance or a demanding attitude is indicative of people who need to put others down in order to feel good about themselves.

Finally, children learn in a variety of ways and each has different strengths. Along the way, children have to determine what they are good at and what they are passionate about. Too often children think they know their strengths and weaknesses, but many times, unfortunately, they can be wrong in both cases. The key is to develop strengths and improve weaknesses, which are important in making decisions.

Children need feedback on their performance so they can identify and build on their most valuable strengths. In addition, students should recognize their most dangerous weaknesses.[11] This is a part of developing self-understanding, which is important in furthering education, aspirations, and relating to others. People have to learn how they work to get things done; lack of that knowledge can cause individuals to fall short. A corollary issue is for students to learn how they learn.

Parents and teachers can help children learn more effectively. Lifelong learning has always been a constant in pursuing purpose and the good life. Thinking otherwise places people in self-restrictive circumstances.

Sometimes, schools expect all children to learn the same way. Reading or listening, working with others or working alone, working under pressure or in highly structured contexts are questions that raise awareness of how people learn best.

Children also must define their values as they move through school. Everyone has to make decisions, and the values for making them should be in harmony with who they are as a person.

In every issue, responsibility is at the core. Responsibility for character, behavior, decisions, fairness, and others are at the essence of a successful life. Responsibility for pursuing ambition and significance, and doing so with integrity to values and respecting the dignity and worth of others, is essential for a life of meaning.

Parents and teachers must model behavior that engages with the world's opportunities and challenges. Then children will learn, and through trying and overcoming, they will find meaning and happiness that becomes a reality, not just a motto or an empty maxim.

POINTS TO REMEMBER

- A victimhood culture destroys give-and-take dialogue and turns it into a "we versus they" society.
- Researchers identify children who can and cannot deal with pressure in stressful circumstances: they are metaphorically called dandelions and orchids, respectively.

- Our society is not a greenhouse free of conflict, pressure, or stress. Cohesive and adaptive families can help children to apply their capabilities to circumstances.
- Society is a chaotic system that doesn't always follow a linear path: relatively small changes and differences can create unexpected major outcomes—the butterfly effect.
- People have imagination, ingenuity, intelligence, and free will from which to respond to what life brings. An internal locus of control enables individuals to develop plans, strategies, and ideas to respond to conditions in change.
- Survivors have a positive perspective and self-reflect to determine how events occurred and what they can do to influence or avert them.
- "Knowing thyself" and self-assessment are essentials in developing self-awareness, self-management, social consciousness, and managing relationships.
- Finding purpose in life answers the question "Why am I here?": it clarifies an individual's calling.
- Responsibilities lie at the core of a successful life through character, behavior, decisions, and integrity to principle.

NOTES

1. Douglas Belkin, "College Faculty's New Focus: Don't Offend," *Wall Street Journal*, February 27, 2017, https://www.wsj.com/articles/college-faculty's-new-focus-don't-offend-1488200404.

2. Arthur C. Brooks, "The Real Victims of Victimhood," *New York Times*, December 26, 2015, https://www.nytimes.com/2015/12/27/opinion/sunday/the-real-victims-of-victimhood.html?_r=0.

3. Neil A. Lewis, "Justice Thomas Assails Victim Mentality," *New York Times*, May 17, 1994, http://www.nytimes.com/1994/05/17/us/justice-thomas-assails-victim-mentality.html.

4. Bruce J. Ellis and W. Thomas Boyce, "Biological Sensitivity to Context," *Development and Psychopathology* 17, no. 2 (June 2005): 271–301.

5. Robert S. Kaplan, "What to Ask the Person in the Mirror," in *On Managing Yourself*, ed. Harvard Business Review (Boston: Harvard University Press, 2010), Reprint R0701H.

6. Daniel Goleman, Richard Boyatzis, and Annie McKee, "Primal Leadership: The Hidden Driver of Great Performance," in *On Managing Yourself*, ed. Harvard Business Review (Boston: Harvard University Press, 2010), Reprint R011C.

7. Ibid.

8. Richard J. Leider, *The Power of Purpose* (New York: MJF Books, 1997), 40.

9. Clayton M. Christensen, "How Will You Measure Your Life?" in *On Managing Yourself*, ed. Harvard Business Review (Boston: Harvard University Press, 2010), Reprint 1007B.

10. Ibid.

11. Peter F. Drucker, "Managing Oneself," in *On Managing Yourself*, ed. Harvard Business Review (Boston: Harvard University Press, 2010), Reprint R0501K.

Chapter Eleven

What Is at Stake?

"The barnacle is confronted with an existential decision about where it's going to live. Once it decides . . . it spends the rest of its life with his head cemented to a rock. For a good many of us, it comes to that. A lot of people stop learning and growing far earlier than they should." —John Gardner

"I learned this . . . that if one advances confidently in the direction of his dreams, and endeavors to live the life which he has imagined, he will meet with success unexpected in common hours." —Henry David Thoreau

Heartbreak! Heartbreak is the loss of aspirations and seeing no individual recourse to make a difference: to give up and fall into victimhood but still have dreams dancing in your mind. These individuals imprison their potential and aspirations.

A mental prison can be as bad as a physical prison. When you are trapped in a mental prison, the crippling idea or feeling robs you of all joy and freedom. You can see and feel little else. Your mind becomes a small room without light. You turn the wild mystery of your own mind into a shabby, negative little room; the windows are blocked, and there is no door. The mental prison is devastatingly lonely. It is a sorrowful place, because ultimately it is you who locks yourself up within a demented idea or feeling.[1]

Mental prisons are filled with laments about what might have been scribbled on the cell walls of passive and cold fatalism. Wonder and joy die a slow death at what could have been. The sadness and tragic deadening of initiative and creativity comes from the fact that it is self-determined and self-inflicted.

The tragedy doesn't have to happen. Each person has to decide how he or she responds to life and the circumstances it brings. Life is short—but is full of potential and purpose. Parents and educators should not let children waste it by becoming self-designated prisoners unable to live, flourish, and address challenges.

All children have dreams. If adults allow children to fall into a victim mentality, then children will never fulfill their version of themselves or their unique story. Only resentment and bitterness will follow later in life at the lost possibilities. In essence, children who assume victim mentality cement their heads to the metaphorical rock with the reciprocal and inevitable stunted growth and narrow perspective.

Everyone—parents, teachers, relatives, and others—must work together to help open gates, to help children see different viewpoints, to help them find themselves, to answer the question, "Who am I?" and to guide them with integrity to positive values and principles in words and deeds.

Children need active guidance and feedback with care and mindfulness. Nurturing is not a benign activity where the mantra "anything goes" is operative. Values and ethics place limits on actions and behavior, and children have to understand that as they define who they are.

Helping children find themselves is not a game of statistical analysis. Discovery of and faith in oneself come from loving connections with significant others that provide insight and understanding. Sometimes these connections are not dramatic events but quiet words that have an emotional impact and remain poignant with children for a lifetime. In schools today, the emphasis is on skills, technology, and assessments. Skills and content are important—but attitude and character create the foundation for their application.

Attitude can diminish or sidetrack the application of skills and knowledge, putting them on the shelf of indifference or in the darkness of destructive ethical and moral behavior. Character, attitudes, and principles are interwoven in the application of intelligence and knowledge.

REALITY

Children of all ages must understand that the world does not revolve around them. They must realize they are part of the world and can contribute to it through their talents, perspectives, humanity, and heart. It takes hard work and commitment. There are no special people who will not face travails and risks.

Children are unique and distinctive, but they are not better than others—they are not "special." If they want to make the world a better place, they must participate. Resilience and determination are absolute necessities to go through life and to work their way through family, personal, and career issues.

Being response-able does not mean that things are always going to go their way. There will be disappointments, but those times also present opportunities. Sometimes great moments are born out of great difficulty. Even defeat can open doors to great achievements.

Life is not always totally rational. Well-planned, logical, and thoughtful events run into the "nonrational" social, political, and interpersonal realities. However, responsibility rests on each individual's shoulders. Skeptical and critical thinking is required as individuals work their way through life. Even so, people are still accountable for their choices and behavior.

Children must be held accountable. One misconception some children and parents have is that everything is negotiable. Actually there are non-negotiables in life. Principles and values are markers against which behavior and character are measured and limited. Ethics raise issues that require thought and debate and often create conflict. The standards adopted that guide life are important because they are the foundation for the establishment of individual integrity and set limitations on bargaining and nuance.

Understanding the principles undergirding life is a critical aspect of answering the "Who am I?" question with which all people wrestle. What people stand for defines them, and if their behavior or words betray those values and principles, then they lose credibility. Without credibility, respect, trust, and integrity are lost—all of them matter in work, citizenship, and relationships. If people are to maintain their good character, then not everything is negotiable.

Children want things—material goods—as do many adults. Tangibles are comforting, but when all is said and done in life, the intangibles matter more. The Harvard Grant Study, a seventy-five-year longitudinal study of adult development, found that what matters in life is love and relationships.[2] They lead to happiness through a connection to others and purpose that brings satisfaction and meaning.

Happiness, meaning, and love are those intangibles people live and die for. They are priceless and cannot be bought. They are the result of knowledge, understanding, compassion, and courage. Wisdom is more than being smart and moves beyond the superficial to the depths of understanding life beyond self-interest and ego.

With autonomy come responsibility and accountability. Implications are tied to decisions, which do not have a benign impact on self and others. Even playing the victim is a decision with consequences for the individual and others. Eventually, running away or deflecting responsibility catches up to people. Every adult role carries responsibility.

Responding intelligently and passionately to life is what makes individuals unique: they control their thoughts, attitudes, and reactions. Encasing individual potential and talent in the victim mentality prison cell does not lead to meaning or a life that is creative and flourishing. It simply leaves an emptiness that hollows out a person's self, potential, and personality.

WHAT TO DO!

Dietrich Bonhoeffer states, "Time lost is time in which we have failed to live a full human life, gain experience, learn, create, enjoy, and suffer; it is time that is not been filled up, but left empty."[3]

Time is a precious gift. Adults generally know life's fragility and the value and unpredictability of the time individuals have. Many teens and young adults think that they are invincible and immortal. Time seems like an endless commodity, but it is not and to waste it is a self-destructive behavior and deeply damaging.

Adults must model behavior if they are to help children. Actions, as the old adage asserts, speak louder than words. As children grow, they seek to see if parents', teachers', and adults' actions match the rhetoric. Setting an example, even if it curtails the children's desire, is the right thing to do.

In working with children, accepting excuses from them is not appropriate: it is a form of manipulation that in the long-term has destructive consequences. It also is a form of deceit and compromises their standing and integrity in living up to their obligations. Letting kids "off the hook" and accepting excuses affects their expectations for the future, as well as their mindset toward life.

Mindsets—optimistic or pessimistic—are observed by children each day. Parents and other adults are important teachers. A "can-do" rather than a "woe-is-me" attitude is important. Parents who blame others or take negative, pessimistic stances are sending a message to their children. Circumstances happen, but being victimized by them and being unable to respond is a choice, and blaming and excuses are destructive.

With an uncertain and ever-changing future, a positive mindset is the only approach that will help children adapt resiliently to it, whatever transpires. Demonstrating resilience is a great lesson. Parents and others can help children by supporting them at tough times to help them get through. This does not mean jumping in and saving the day, but it does mean sitting and listening, helping them determine why things happened as they did, and defining what options and opportunities are available to them.

Failure too often is always painted as a disaster to kids. But it happens to everyone at some point in time. Adults who provide guidance and support when children face times when things go awry are invaluable resources. What happened, why, and what recourse is available is an important step. In addition, determining what was learned in the situation or effort is extremely valuable so that it can be avoided in the future. Children must determine what opportunities are available from the circumstances that they face.

The travesty is that avoiding responsibility and engaging in self-pity and fear of failure wastes the potential of a unique life. Engaging in self-indulgent manipulation of family, friends, and others is not a solution. The individual loses the possibility for growth and the pursuit of meaning and purpose, and society is deprived of distinctive talent and potential.

Complacent or fearful people who fail to answer the call cannot survive and contribute to their family or the greater good. If allowed to happen, then children will not fully participate in creating their own future and living freely.

Life is to be lived actively with virtue and significance. When reflecting on life, the importance of commitment and responsible action dedicated to constructive values and principles becomes clear. Character, intelligence, and wisdom should guide the choices necessary to realize a fulfilling and meaningful life.

Maturity brings independence and options. Choices arise and people should make them based on the philosophical dispositions: values, principles, and ethics. Discussing the philosophical interpretations and impact of events and propositions is important. When things are unclear, as in conflict, people should always fall back on the philosophical beliefs to guide their decisions and conduct.

Commitment to a cause for good versus commitment to family is a conflict demonstrated in history. Helping children think deeply about these issues and the possible options can help them become active players rather than passive victims who forgo responsibility to address issues.

SOCIETY

Society, particularly in a democracy, depends on individuals fulfilling their potential and contributing their skills. Adopting a victim mentality is not simply a personal concern. In actuality, it affects the larger picture, particularly our free society. Individuals who believe in their own helplessness and accept and bask in it are a serious problem.

Communities and government rely on involvement and commitment by citizens. Helpless indifference is an anathema in a democracy. Freedom is an active principle that requires participation and contribution by all. History has illustrated governments who were allowed to pursue destructive paths because people sat silent and did not get involved.

Individuals are capable of compassion and indifference, of "ennobling" life and disfiguring it.[4] Maintaining great societies can only be done through freedom and the belief in the strengths of independence and actions of the common citizen. Each citizen has an obligation to look beyond self and see the gift of freedom and the uniqueness to contribute to greater possibilities and achievements. Basically, people are called to affect their own welfare through thoughtful participation in the democratic process.

In a great sense, the future success of the United States depends on individuals who believe in the virtues of the American Dream—liberty, justice, equality, and the common good. A nation of dreamers can do great things. Indifferent self-victimization produces nothing.

Imagination, morality, and perseverance are the principles that have produced great things and have sustained a government and society that many said was not possible. While people can be deceived or distracted, they are not helpless.[5]

A major attitude that all parents and adults must instill in children is that they are not helpless. They are responsible and response-able to resiliently address the issues they are going to face in life. Two quotes address this attitude:

- Joseph Campbell states, "Life is without meaning. You bring the meaning to it. The meaning of life is whatever you ascribe it to be. Being alive is the meaning."[6]
- John O'Donohue wrote, "There are no manuals for the construction of the individual you would like to become. You are the only one who can decide this and take up the lifetime of work that it demands. This is such a wonderful privilege and such an exciting adventure. To grow into the person that your deepest longing desires is a great blessing. . . . The gift of life is given to us for ourselves and also to bring peace, courage, and compassion to others."[7]

POINTS TO REMEMBER

- People build mental prisons that restrict their talent and ability to live and experience life.
- Parents, teachers, and others should open gates to help children gain perspective, find their calling, and live with integrity.
- Character, attitudes, and principles are interwoven in the application of intelligence and knowledge.
- Children have to learn that the world does not revolve around them: they are unique, not special.
- Intangibles in life bring more happiness and meaning than tangible things.
- Society and democratic government rely on responsible and action-oriented citizens.

NOTES

1. John O'Donohue, *Eternal Echoes* (New York: HarperCollins, 1999), 107.
2. George E. Vaillant, *Aging Well* (Boston: Little, Brown and Company, 2002).
3. Dietrich Bonhoeffer, *Letters and Papers from Prison* (New York: Touchstone, 1997), 3.
4. Norman Cousins, *Human Options* (New York: W. W. Norton & Company, 1981), 58–61.
5. Ibid., 68.
6. Joseph Campbell, *Joseph Campbell: Reflections on the Art of Living*, ed. Diane K. Osbon (New York: Harper Perennial, 1991), 16.
7. O'Donohue, *Eternal Echoes*, 102.

Bibliography

BOOKS

Adams, James Truslow. *The Epic of America*. New Brunswick, NJ: Transaction, 2012.
Adler, Mortimer J. *Reforming Education*. Edited by Geraldine van Doren. New York: Macmillan, 1977.
Badaracco, Joseph L. *Defining Moments*. Boston: Harvard Business School Press, 1997.
Bonhoeffer, Dietrich. *Letters and Papers from Prison*. New York: Touchstone, 1997.
Botstein, Leon. *Jefferson's Children*. New York: Doubleday, 1997.
Brooks, David. *The Road to Character*. New York: Random House, 2015.
Brooks, Robert, and Sam Goldstein. *The Power of Resilience: Achieving Balance, Confidence, and Personal Strength in Your Life*. New York: McGraw-Hill Education, 2004.
———. *Raising Resilient Children*. New York: McGraw Hill, 2001.
———. *Resilient Children: Fostering Strength, Hope and Optimism in Your Child*. New York: McGraw-Hill Education, 2001.
Campbell, Joseph. *Joseph Campbell: Reflections on the Art of Living*. Edited by Diane K. Osbon. New York: Harper Perennial, 1991.
Christensen, Clayton M. "How Will You Measure Your Life?" In *On Managing Yourself*, edited by *Harvard Business Review*, Reprint R1007B. Boston: Harvard University Press, 2010. Originally published in *Harvard Business Review*, July/August 2010.
Cousins, Norman. *Human Options*. New York: W. W. Norton and Company, 1981.
Covey, Stephen. *The 7 Habits of Highly Effective People*. New York: RossettaBooks, 2013.
Csikszentmihalyi, Mihaly. *Flow*. New York: HarperCollins, 2008.
———. *A Life Worth Living*. New York: Oxford University Press, 2006.
Drucker, Peter F. "Managing Oneself." In *On Managing Yourself*, edited by *Harvard Business Review*, Reprint R0501K. Boston: Harvard University Press, 2010. Originally published in *Harvard Business Review*, January 1999.
Dweck, Carol. *Mindset: New Psychology of Success*. New York: Random House, 2006.
Elmore, Tim. *Artificial Maturity*. San Francisco: Jossey-Bass, 2012.
Erikson, Erik H. *Childhood and Society*. New York: W. W. Norton and Company, 1964.
———. *Identity: Youth and Crisis*. New York: W. W. Norton and Company, 1968.
Etzioni, Amitai. *The Spirit of Community*. New York: Crown, 1993.
Frankl, Viktor. *Man's Search for Meaning*. New York: Washington Square Press, 1984.
———. *The Will to Meaning*. New York: Penguin, 1988.
Friedman, Thomas L. *The World Is Flat*. New York: Farrar, Strauss, and Giroux, 2005.
Gardner, John. *Excellence*. New York: W. W. Norton and Company, 1984.

———. *Living, Leading, and the American Dream*. San Francisco: Jossey-Bass, 2003.
Glasser, William. *Choice Theory: A New Psychology for Personal Freedom*. New York: HarperCollins, 2010.
Goens, George A. *The Fog of Reform*. Lanham, MD: Rowman & Littlefield, 2016.
———. *The Promise of Living*. San Francisco: Turning Stone Press, 2013.
———. *Soft Leadership for Hard Times*. Lanham, MD: Rowman & Littlefield, 2005.
Goens, George A., and Phil Streifer. *Straitjacket*. Lanham, MD: Rowman & Littlefield, 2013.
Goleman, Daniel. *Emotional Intelligence*. New York: Random House, 2012.
Goleman, Daniel, Richard Boyatzis, and Annie McKee. "Primal Leadership: The Hidden Driver of Great Performance." In *On Managing Yourself*, edited by *Harvard Business Review*, Reprint R011C. Boston: Harvard University Press, 2010. Originally published in *Harvard Business Review*, December 2001.
Gough, Russell W. *Character Is Destiny*. Rocklin, CA: Prima Publishing, 1997.
Greenleaf, Robert K. *Servant Leadership*. New York: Paulist Press, 1997.
Gurian, Michael. *A Fine Young Man*. New York: Tarcher Putnam, 1998.
Harris, Maxine. *The Loss That Is Forever*. New York: Penguin, 1996.
Harris, Monica J. *Bullying, Rejection, and Peer Victimization: A Social Cognitive Neuroscience Perspective*. New York: Springer, 2009.
Hart, Gary. *The Good Fight*. New York: Random House, 1993.
Havel, Vaclav. *The Art of the Impossible*. New York: Knopf, 1997.
Hunter, James D. *The Death of Character*. New York: Basic Books, 2000.
Kaplan, Robert S. "What to Ask the Person in the Mirror." In *On Managing Yourself*, edited by *Harvard Business Review*, Reprint R0701H. Boston: Harvard University Press, 2010. Originally published in *Harvard Business Review*, January 2007.
Keyes, Corey L. M., and Jonathan Haidt, eds. *Flourishing: Positive Psychology and the Life Well-Lived*. Washington, DC: American Psychological Association, 2002.
Kofman, Fred. *Conscious Business: How to Build Value through Values*. Boulder, CO: Sounds True, 2006.
Leider, Richard J. *The Power of Purpose*. New York: MJF Books, 1997.
Lickona, Thomas. *Character Matters*. New York: Touchstone, 2004.
Long, Jody E., Nicholas J. Long, and Signe Whitson. *The Angry Smile: The Psychology of Passive-Aggressive Behavior in Families, Schools, and Workplaces* Austin, TX: PRO-ED, 2008.
Lythcott-Haims, Julie. *How to Raise an Adult: Break Free of the Overparenting Trap and Prepare Your Kid for Success*. New York: Henry Holt and Company, 2015.
Metaxas, Eric. *Bonhoeffer: Pastor, Martyr, Prophet, Spy*. Nashville: Thomas Nelson, 2010.
Moore, Thomas. *Care of the Soul*. New York: HarperPerennial, 1992.
Nair, Keshavan. *A Higher Standard of Leadership*. San Francisco: Berrett-Koehler, 1994.
O'Brien, William J. *Character at Work*. New York: Paulist Press, 2008.
O'Donohue, John. *Eternal Echoes*. New York: HarperCollins, 1999.
O'Toole, James. *Creating the Good Life*. New York: Rodale, 2005.
Peck, M. Scott. *The Road Less Traveled*. New York: Simon & Schuster, 1978.
Peterson, Christopher, and Lisa M. Bassio. *Health and Optimism*. New York: The Free Press, 1991.
Peterson, Christopher, and Martin E. P. Seligman. *Character Strengths and Virtues*. New York: Oxford University Press, 2004.
Peterson, Christopher, Steven F. Maier, and Martin E. P. Seligman. *Learned Helplessness*. New York: Oxford University Press, 1993.
Pruett, Kyle D. *Fatherneed*. New York: Broadway Books, 2000.
———. *Me, Myself, and I*. New York: Gotthard Press, 1999.
Robinson, Ken, and Lou Aronica. *Finding Your Element*. New York: Penguin, 2013.
Rose, Mike. *Why School?* New York: The New Press, 2009.
Seligman, Martin E. P. *Flourish*. New York: Atria, 2011.
———. *Helplessness*. San Francisco: W. H. Freeman and Company, 1975.
Siebert, Al. *The Resiliency Advantage*. San Francisco: Barrett-Koehler, 2005.
Tartaglia, Louis A. *Flawless*. New York: William Morrow and Company, 1999.

Thoreau, Henry David. *Walden and Civil Disobedience*. New York: Penguin, 1983.
Vaillant, George. *Aging Well*. Boston: Little, Brown and Company, 2002.
———. *Spiritual Evolution*. New York: Broadway Books, 2008.
———. *The Wisdom of the Ego*. Cambridge, MA: Harvard University Press, 1993.
Whyte, David. *The Heart Aroused*. New York: Currency Doubleday, 1994.

JOURNALS, MULTIMEDIA, AND ONLINE RESOURCES

Baumeister, Roy F., Kathleen D. Vohs, Jennifer L. Aaker, and Emily N. Garbinsky. "Some Key Differences between a Happy Life and a Meaningful Life." *The Journal of Positive Psychology* 8, no. 6 (August 30, 2013): 505–16.
Becker-Phelps, Leslie. "6 Signs of 'Victim' Mentality." *Relationships* (blog). WebMD. May 18, 2016. http://blogs.webmd.com/art-of-relationships/2016/05/6-signs-of-victim-mentality.html.
Belkin, Douglas. "College Faculty's New Focus: Don't Offend," *Wall Street Journal*. February 27, 2017. www.wsj.com/articles/college-faculty's-new-focus-don't-offend-1488200404.
Bonde, Sheila, and Paul Firenza. "A Framework for Making Ethical Decisions." Brown University. May 2013. https://www.brown.edu/academics/science-and-technology-studies/sites/brown.edu.academics.science-and-technology-studies/files/uploads/Framework.pdf.
Bradley-Geist, Jill C., and Julie B. Olson-Buchanan. "Helicopter Parents: An Examination of the Correlates of Over-parenting College Students." *Education and Training* 56, no. 4 (2014): 314–28.
Brooks, Arthur C. "The Real Victims of Victimhood." *New York Times*. December 26, 2015. https://www.nytimes.com/2015/12/27/opinion/sunday/the-real-victims-of-victimhood.html?_r=0.
Centers for Disease Control and Prevention. "Health-Related Quality of Life: Well-Being Concepts." Last modified May 31, 2016. https://www.cdc.gov/hrqol/wellbeing.htm.
Daniel, Kerilyn. "What Is a Good Life?" Distinguished major thesis, University of Virginia, 2009.   docplayer.net/12588778-What-is-the-good-life-a-place-for-positive-psychology-kerilyn-daniel-distinguished-majors-thesis-university-of-virginia.html.
Diaz, Lisette Candia. "I'm an undocumented Harvard grad. The election has left me broken." *PostPartisan Opinion* (blog). *Washington Post*. November 25, 2016. https://www.washingtonpost.com/blogs/post-partisan/wp/2016/11/25/im-an-undocumented-harvard-grad-the-election-has-left-me-broken/.
Ellis, Bruce J., and W. Thomas Boyce. "Biological Sensitivity to Context." *Development and Psychopathology* 17, no. 2 (June 2005): 271–301.
Finn, Jeremy D., and Donald A. Rock. "Academic Success among Students at Risk for School Failure." *Journal of Applied Psychology* 82, no. 2 (1997): 231–34.
Fitzel, Rob. "The Nine Types of Students." The Enneagram. 2001. http://www.fitzel.ca/enneagram/education/index.html.
Friedersdorf, Conor. "The Rise of Victimhood Culture." *The Atlantic*. September 11, 2015. https://www.theatlantic.com/politics/archive/2015/09/the-rise-of-victimhood-culture/404794/.
Gardner, Howard. "Re-Inventing the Wheel in the Study of Human Character." *The Good Blog*. The Good Project. April 2004. http://www.thegoodproject.org/re-inventing-the-wheel-in-the-study-of-human-character/.
Gray, Alex. "The 10 Skills You Need to Thrive in the Fourth Industrial Revolution." World Economic Forum. January 19, 2016. https://www.weforum.org/agenda/2016/01/the-10-skills-you-need-to-thrive-in-the-fourth-industrial-revolution.
Jarrett, Robin L. "Successful Parenting in High-Risk Neighborhoods." *The Future of Children* 9, no. 2 (Fall 1999): 45–50.
Kaufman, Scott Barry. "The Differences between Happiness and Meaning in Life." *Scientific American Blog Network*. January 30, 2016. https://blogs.scientificamerican.com/beautiful-minds/the-differences-between-happiness-and-meaning-in-life.

Kets de Vries, Manfred F. R. "Are You a Victim of the Victim Syndrome?" Faculty and research working paper. INSEAD. 2012. https://sites.insead.edu/facultyresearch/research/doc.cfm?did=50114.

Koestner, Richard, Nancy Otis, Theodore A. Powers, Luc Pelletier, and Hugo Gagnon. "Autonomous Motivation, Controlled Motivation, and Goal Progress." *Journal of Personality* 76, no. 5 (October 2008): 1201–30.

Lehman, James. "I'm a Victim, so the Rules Don't Apply to Me." Empowering Parents. August 2, 2012. https://www.empoweringparents.com/article/im-a-victim-so-the-rules-dont-apply-to-me-how-to-stop-victim-thinking-in-kids/.

Lewis, Neil A. "Justice Thomas Assails Victim Mentality." *New York Times*. May 17, 1994. http://www.nytimes.com/1994/05/17/us/justice-thomas-assails-victim-mentality.html.

Lucas, Suzanne. "How to Achieve the American Dream." CBS MoneyWatch. June 6, 2004. http://www.cbsnews.com/news/how-to-revive-your-american-dream/.

Lukianoff, Greg, and Jonathan Haidt. "The Coddling of the American Mind." *The Atlantic*. September 2015. http://www.theatlantic.com/magazine/archive/2015/09/the-coddling-of-the-american-mind/399356/.

MacKay, Ross. "Family Resilience and Good Child Outcomes: An Overview of the Research Literature." *Social Policy Journal of New Zealand* 20 (June 2003): 98–118.

Online Etymology Dictionary. www.etymonline.com/index.php?term=autonomy.

Pala, Ayner. "The Need for Character Education." *International Journal of Social Sciences and Humanity Studies* 3, no. 2 (2011).

Park, Nansook, and Christopher Peterson. "Character Strengths: Research and Practice." *Journal of College and Character* 10, no. 4 (April 2009): 1–10.

Parker, Kim. "Families May Differ, but They Share Common Values on Parenting." Pew Research Center. September 18, 2014. http://www.pewresearch.org/fact-tank/2014/09/18/families-may-differ-but-they-share-common-values-on-parenting/.

Parncutt, Richard. "Victim Mentality, Self-Efficacy, and Politics." September 2015. http://www.parncutt.org/victim.html.

Pew Research Center. "Parenting in America." December 17, 2015. http://www.pewsocialtrends.org/2015/12/17/parenting-in-america/.

Rand Corporation. "The Future at Work—Trends and Implications." 2004. http://www.rand.org/pubs/research_briefs/RB5070/index1.html.

Rowling, J. K. "The Fringe Benefits of Failure, and the Importance of Imagination." Speech, Cambridge, MA, June 5, 2008. *Harvard Gazette*. http://news.harvard.edu/gazette/story/2008/06/text-of-j-k-rowling-speech/.

Smith, Aaron. "AI, Robotics, and the Future of Jobs." Pew Research Center. August 6, 2014. http://www.pewinternet.org/2014/08/06/future-of-jobs/.

Stallone, Sylvester. *Rocky Balboa*. Beverly Hills, CA: Metro-Goldwyn-Mayer, 2006.

Sternberg, Robert J. "Creativity Is a Habit." *Education Week*. February 21, 2006. http://www.edweek.org/ew/articles/2006/02/22/24sternberg.h25.html.

Swanson, Jodi, Carlos Valiente, Kathryn Lemery-Chalfant, and T. Caitlin O'Brien. "Predicting Early Adolescents' Academic Achievement, Social Competence, and Physical Health from Parenting, Ego Resilience, and Engagement Coaching." *Journal of Early Adolescence* 31, no. 4 (2011): 548–76.

Zitek, Emily M., Alexander H. Jordan, Benoit Monin, and Frederick R. Leach. "Victim Entitlement to Behave Selfishly." *Journal of Personality and Social Psychology* 98, no. 2 (2010): 245–55.

Index

accountability, 17, 19, 28, 29–31, 31, 33, 42, 50, 53, 57, 62, 68, 77–78, 80, 92, 95–96, 97, 119
active listening, 81–82, 84, 85
Adams, James Truslow, x
agape, 95
American Dream, ix–x; Declaration of Independence, x; democratic society, 6; pursuit of happiness, x
artificial intelligence, 73, 74
Autonomy, 10, 18, 28–29, 29, 38, 39, 53, 57, 62, 103, 106, 119
autotelic self, 65

Balboa, Rocky, 48–49
Bassio, Lisa, 20–21
behavior: passive aggressive, 16–17, 22, 25, 27, 34, 41, 104; proactive, 29, 68
being and doing, 61–62, 68
Bonhoeffer, Dietrich, 28, 120
Botstein, Leon, 84
Bower, Claire, 54–56
Brooks, David, 51, 105
Brooks, Herb, 47–48
bullying, 20
butterfly effect, 105, 110, 116

chaos theory, 110
character, 3, 4, 10, 46–54, 51, 53; blaming, 78; destiny, 4, 51, 53, 82, 95; hidden curriculum, 53; philosophy of life, 51; responsibility, 27–31; strengths, 51–52, 52, 54, 56, 57, 79, 85; temperance, 51, 53, 85
children : anxiety, 2, 31, 41, 47–49, 54, 92, 93; cognitive development, 13; dandelions, 109, 115; entitled, 83, 92, 108; orchids, 107, 109, 115; peers, 14, 42, 57, 63, 82, 90, 94; resilience, 38, 60, 65–66, 66, 88–89, 90, 92, 96–97
choices, 18–19
citizenship, 5, 6, 7
Comer, James, 1
common good, 6
common man, x
consciousness, 9
controllables, xi
core values, 7, 35, 79
courage, 8–9, 22, 54, 66, 79, 82
Cousins, Norman, 1, 18
creativity, 8
Csikszentmihalyi, Mihaly, 19, 40, 65

de Vries, Ket, 15, 16

educated person, 5–8
education, 1, 2; change, 4, 5; class size, 83; cognitive processing, 35, 43; cognitive skills, 5, 71, 85; critical thinking, 6–7; education and values, 1, 3; education spiritual dimension, 8, 100, 113; fine arts, 8; Pew Research, 2–3, 5; purpose

in life, 8, 37, 40, 43, 44, 101, 112–113; skeptical thinking, 6, 7; World Economic Forum, 73
Einstein, 71, 107
emotional intelligence, 18–19, 23, 73, 112
ethics, 4, 5, 62–63

failure, fear of, 12, 40, 46, 59, 77, 91, 121
family and,: character, 52, 53, 56–57; belief system, 89; culture, 89, 95, 97, 114; resilience, 88–89, 96, 97; structure, 87–88; values, 30
flow, 36, 40–41, 104
frames of mind, 20–21, 80
Frankl, Viktor. E., 9, 36–37, 37, 39
Friedman, Thomas, 71

Gardner, John, xi, 22, 43, 59, 117
Goleman, Daniel, 18–19, 41
goodness, 3, 37, 53, 62, 102, 113
Gough, Russell, 51
Ground Hog Day, 15
guilt trips, 17

happiness, x, xi, 6, 8
Harris, Maxine, 95
Havel, Vaclav, 50
Heart, Gary, 4
Heraclitus, 53
heroes, 46

imagination, 8, 71, 93, 110, 116, 122
integrity, 7, 8, 28, 30, 32, 47, 51, 60, 104, 112, 114, 119, 122

Jefferson, Thomas, 3, 87
joy, 42, 44, 94, 100, 104, 117, 122
justice, ix, 3, 4, 5, 45, 50; character, 13, 35, 51, 53, 57, 62, 85

Kaufman, Scott, 35
King, Martin Luther, 45
Kofman, Fred, 17, 28, 66

life : flourish, 100, 102, 103, 104, 105–106; languish, 102, 103, 105, 106, 111
life-long learning, 5, 115

locus of control, 16, 22, 23, 34, 63, 110, 111, 116

Madison Avenue, 46
man's search for meaning, 36–37
manipulation, 33, 46, 120, 121
Mann, Horace, 3
Maslow, Abraham, 36
maturity, xi, 18, 28, 44, 68, 75, 79, 86; emotional maturity, 34; schools, 82; self-management, 109, 112; wisdom, 42
mental prisons, 117–122
mindfulness, 7, 8, 13, 29, 72, 118
mindsets, 34, 52, 57, 66–67, 89, 90, 96–97, 104, 120
Moore, Thomas, 11
motivation, 27, 78; autonomous, 92; controlled, 92

need hierarchy, 36

O'Brien, William, 82
O'Donoghue, John, 9
obligations, x, 27, 28, 31, 68, 72
Olympic 1980 Hockey Team, 47–48, 67
optimism and pessimism, 13–15, 20–21, 85, 103
over parenting, 91, 92, 97, 108

parents, xi, 2, 90–97; accountability, 95–96; attitudes, 2; collaborators, 96; death of, 15, 54, 55, 57, 75; helicopter, 91, 92; parenting styles, 30; nurturing, 94, 118; overprotective, 88, 91, 92; positive, 96–97; style and victim mentality, 93–95
perseverance, 9, 35, 67, 89, 103, 122
persistence, xi, 14, 63, 64, 79, 80
pessimists, 12, 13, 15, 20, 41
Peterson and Seligman, 51, 52, 79
Peterson, Christopher, 20
Pew Research Center, 2–3, 5, 87, 88
polestars, 47, 80, 81, 104
Pruett, 90
purpose in life, 8, 37, 40, 43, 44, 101, 112–113

Rand Corporation, 5
resilience, 60, 65–67, 118

response-able, xi, 28–30, 50
Roosevelt, Eleanor, 45, 94
Roosevelt, Franklin D., 46
Roosevelt, Theodore, 71

school culture, 114
self-actualization, 36, 104
self-awareness, 9, 66
self-control, 52
self-concept, 8, 10, 17, 78
self-destructive behavior, x, xi, 18, 22, 64, 77, 78
self-efficacy, x, 21, 27, 63–64, 66, 68, 92, 97, 110
self-esteem, 27, 32, 34, 49, 51, 59, 114
self-pity, xi, 21, 46, 85, 121
self-regulation, 64, 68, 79
self-reliance, x, 42, 54
self-understanding, 8, 10, 43, 51, 103, 115; character, 53, 85; success, 80, 100; tragedies, 53–54, 95, 117
stewardship, 2

Tartaglia, Louis, 78

technology, 5, 6, 30, 73, 118
thinking errors, 95–96, 97
Thoreau, Henry David, 117

Vaillant, George, 65
victim mentality, xi, 15, 16–18, 19, 22, 106, 118, 119; being and doing, 61–62; ethics, 62–64; family, 34, 41; languishing, 102–104; outlook on life, 12–13, 33–34, 41–43; parents, 93–95, 96–97; students, 77–78, 91; versus bullying, 20
virtues, 4, 35–36, 42, 50, 51, 53, 63, 104, 106, 121, 122
Voltaire, 12

Whyte, David, 49
Winthrop, John, 45
wisdom, 4, 6, 36, 38, 40, 42, 43, 51, 54, 57, 67, 72, 79, 85, 94, 104, 106, 119, 121
World Economic Forum, 73

Yeats, William Butler, 3